A
GATHERING
AT THE
RIVER

A GATHERING AT THE RIVER

Stories From a Life in the Foreign Service
by
Fred Godsey

MARKGRAF
PUBLICATIONS GROUP
PO BOX 936
MENLO PARK, CA

Copyright 1989 by Markgraf Publications Group,
a division of The Robots, Inc.

Markgraf Publications Group
a division of The Robots Inc.
P. O. Box 936
Menlo Park, CA 94025

Printed and bound in the United States of America
using premium quality, neutral pH papers

ISBN 0-944109-03-9 Hardcover
      0-944109-04-7 Softcover
Library of Congress Catalog Card Number 88-061315

I respectfully dedicate this work to the memory of my friend, Alajos Pongracz, who was murdered in a communist prison in Budapest, Hungary, in 1952, by agents of the Soviet Union and the communist government of Hungary.

Fred Godsey

Mt. Pleasant, Texas

PREFACE

One can study the art of diplomacy by reading the memoirs of Metternich and Kissinger and emerge with a picture not unlike the impressions of soldiering to be gained from Churchill's famous history of World War II. It is indeed at the top that the important decisions are made, the policies promulgated, the pacts forged. Yet without their people on the front lines, these leaders would have been powerless. Not only would there be no one to execute their orders, but there would be no one to provide them the very information vital to their decisions.

What cartoonist Bill Mauldin did for the American GI in World War II, through his charcoal sketches of the rough-hewn heroes Willy and Joe, Fred Godsey has done for the American Foreign Service officer in this collection of stories.

Fred spent the war years in a South American post, then in effect relieved Willy and Joe after the Nazi surrender in

Europe by fighting a series of desperate battles in the political and bureaucratic trenches of Budapest as the Communists consolidated their hold over Hungary and the rest of Eastern Europe.

As I write this on the forty-second anniversary of Winston Churchill's "Iron Curtain" speech, it occurs to me that Fred was at center stage when that fabled curtain descended. Churchill, of course, was using metaphor, but to Fred the curtain was palpable and intolerable.

Though they saw their friends betrayed and killed or forcibly separated from their families and lovers, though they had to step over corpses to walk to work at the legation in Budapest, though they had to tolerate the personal privations of war's aftermath, Fred and his diplomatic colleagues were every bit as patriotic as Willy and Joe and the real American GIs. Mentally unshaven, a little cynical, perhaps even justifiably hung over—not to mention overworked and underpaid—but with a clear sense of moral purpose that they were the emissaries of a nation that had saved the world from Fascism and simply had to do its best to save it from Communism as the survivors dug out from the ruins.

This is a collection of war stories from the front lines of diplomacy. Each is charged with emotion. Some will make you laugh aloud, some make you fierce with pride, some will make you angry, and some will make you weep. None will leave you unaffected or unimpressed.

These stories may be fictitious, but they are based on actual events viewed from the fabled veranda of American diplomatic missions on two continents. With the toll of American diplomats killed in the line of duty at an intolerable level—some sixty have been assassinated in the last twenty years—no informed person still believes that the life of a Foreign Service officer is confined to parties on that veranda.

The image still holds, however, that diplomacy largely consists of the Secretary of State jetting from one capital to another to force a peace. But just as the airworthiness of the Secretary's plane depends on the professionalism and skill of the ground crew, so does the ability of the treaty to "fly" depend on the competence of the diplomatic ground crew at the respective embassies and back in Washington. In *A Gathering at the River*, Fred Godsey gives us a glimpse of the nuts and bolts of diplomacy, with no regrets for the oil and grease.

Stephen R. Dujack
Editor, Foreign Service Journal, 1981-88

CONTENTS

FAME AND THE FOREIGN SERVICE

FAME AND THE
FOREIGN SERVICE

Let me be quite frank about this. I joined the Foreign Service to seek fame and fortune. I decided to forget fortune after my first paycheck arrived. I hoped that fame, like virtue, would have its own rewards.

For a vice consul, fame is hard to find—I mean real worldwide fame—but I was young and I could see the headlines a few years down the road: "Ambassador Godsey Settles International Dispute" or "Special Envoy Godsey Saves America from Brink of War." Or maybe someday something would be named after me: Say, a treaty; a new city in Africa; an imposing international building; or perhaps a few streets in some world capitals. My imaginative horizons were broad indeed.

Those first years in the Service, I really worked hard. I bombarded the State Department with voluminous reports on anything that moved in my consular district, including

3

one superb document on the value of the *uribu* buzzard as a sanitation adjunct in northern Brazil. I observed diplomatic protocol religiously, but I did have some difficulty remembering which corner of my calling card I was supposed to bend and how many to leave when making courtesy calls. For example, when I arrived at the U. S. embassy in Rome to leave cards, as protocol demanded, I took no chances. I bent all four corners and left a rather large stack of cards, prompting Ambassador Luce's secretary to call me and inquire whether I was running for office.

In expectation of future renown, I cheerfully performed all the lowly tasks assigned to me. I dressed conservatively. I buttered up my superiors. In short, I considered myself an exemplary Foreign Service employee whose coming fame was assured.

Sometime during my second or third year in the Service, I began to pay attention to any news reports relating to embassy or consular personnel. I noticed that these articles almost never mentioned an officer by name, unless he or she got killed, kidnaped, or suffered some other horrendous fate. Instead, they would say "the U. S. ambassador" at such-and-such place, "U. S. official," "an employee of the U. S. consulate," or "a U. S. consul" (more often than not spelled "council"). The one time that I was mentioned was in a news service report originating in Budapest. It concerned the arrest of a U. S. legation secretary by the communist political police. The papers reported that "Vice Consul *Goosy* stated that there is no question that the woman is a citizen of the United States."

I began to have some doubts. Could it be that the individual in the Foreign Service remains an anonymous entity? Does celebrity really exist in the Service? Would fame pass me by?

A few weeks of home leave only served to intensify my uncertainty. My first stop was at a bank in New York to cadge a loan to buy a second-hand car. The sixth assistant vice president examined my beautifully engraved card carefully. The card proclaimed that I was a vice consul of the United States of America. "Hmmm . . . I see," he said. "Well, of course, since you're with the vice squad, I don't think there will be any problem with your loan."

After innumerable instances of being so identified, I tried a new tack: When asked what I did for a living, I would say, "I work for the State Department." Usually the reply was, "What state?" Even a courtesy call on a U. S. senator, at the behest of the State Department, was discouraging. I told the senator that I had just arrived from Budapest. I was certain that he would want to question me about the political and economic situation in Hungary. His only questions were, "What does a vice consul do?" and "How do you like living over there among all those Yugoslavs?" My doubts multiplied, but at least he poured a good bourbon.

In desperation, I considered the history of the Foreign Service. Beginning with Benjamin Franklin, I made a list of famous people who had, at some point in their lives, been in the Service. I eliminated those that achieved stardom *after* leaving the Service. I also struck off those appointed by the president to high posts *after* they had made their marks on the world stage. My remaining list was alarmingly small.

There were many officers, however, who had achieved fame of a sort *within* the Service, even if their exploits had not made them world famous. One had risked his life to snatch an arrested U. S. citizen from the clutches of the communist political police in Hungary. One had effected a truce between rebels and government troops in Mexico. Another had taken charge and organized life in a Japanese prison camp for Americans in the Philippines. The list was very impressive, and stories about these people are still recounted with awe around Foreign Service campfires.

I wondered if perhaps I could get my name on this list. I realized that, given my low rank, the odds were much against it. A new idea came to me when I read a piece about Joel Poinsett, a Foreign Service officer for whom the beautiful poinsettia flowers and plants are named. I would have to search for something which could be named after me— something which future generations and *Webster's Dictionary* would record as being named for Godsey of the U. S. Foreign Service.

My knowledge of plants, especially flowers, being very limited, I consulted an agricultural attache and asked him for a list of exotic plants for which science had not yet found common names. His friendly advice was to lay off the booze. But I was undaunted.

One evening, I sat in a hotel bar in Vienna sipping a dry martini before dinner. As I stirred the little onion with a toothpick, I suddenly realized that I was drinking a Gibson martini—a cocktail bearing the name of a U. S. Foreign Service officer. Aha! That was it! I would concoct a drink, bearing my name, of course, which would become known all over the world. My name would hang behind magnificent bars from Paris to London to Singapore and all points between. I didn't bother to eat dinner but rushed to my apartment to begin my experiments.

I had at home only the usual beverage supply: A few bottles of scotch, a bottle each of gin, vodka, and vermouth, and some liqueur. I decided that the Godsey cocktail should be as simple as possible, so that anyone could make it and think of my name as they did so. Thus I would first try a variation of the Gibson martini. I would substitute a small bulb of garlic, or maybe pickled garlic, for the onion. I wonder if Gibson ever tried that. I suppose he might have, since I didn't feel too well once I had sipped from the first batch and eaten the unpickled garlic. And the next day at the consulate the secretaries wouldn't come near me. But never mind. I pickled some of the garlic and tried again—with the same results.

I realized that I would have to start from scratch. I began assembling one bottle of every type of liquor that I could find in Vienna. This cost two months' salary. Even the tough, worldly-wise sergeant in charge of the PX raised his eyebrows when he saw my purchases. My apartment was soon filled with bottles. Since there was no more space in the kitchen for my housekeeper to do her cooking, she left. But I no longer had time to eat anyway.

Most great discoveries involve many trials and hardships. Everybody knows that. Each time I thought I had the perfect formula, I would invite a few friends over in the evening to sample the new drink. They would invariably say that they liked it. The next evening I would take a small sample to the barman at the French hotel. He would—also invariably—say, "Monsieur, c'est merde!" I didn't give up, though, even after my friends eventually stopped accepting my invitations—some of them were ill.

It took me the greatest part of a year to finally create the Godsey cocktail in its absolute, definitive form. Truth to tell, I had no more friends to try it on, and the Frenchman still said the same thing about it. But it had the stamp of approval of a professional drinker—Private Benjamin Riley of the British Army. Such was Private Riley's renown that he had been imported from London by the British legation solely for the purpose of drinking with the Russians in Austria. He liked the Godsey cocktail. In fact, he liked all of the ingredients, whether mixed or not. He even saved me the trouble of disposing of the contents of all the excess bottles not needed in the experiments.

I didn't bother to consult the Frenchman again. The cocktail was perfect, and I took samples to several of the leading bars in Vienna. I also eventually took a few small bottles to some of the well-known drinking places in London and New York. These trained barmen all said that it was a good drink. Well, they didn't exactly put it that way. What they said was, "Sure, if somebody comes in and asks for this mess, we'll make it. Just leave the recipe."

I'm not stupid enough to give the formula on these pages and have some ambassador make the drink popular at an embassy party, put his name to it, and achieve fame overnight. I resigned from the Foreign Service some time ago to devote my time solely to promoting the cocktail, and I will release the recipe as soon as my name is a household word.

The search for fame and fortune in any profession is not easy. The Godsey cocktail is not yet popular, and there may be those who suspect that my quest for fame has been fruitless. Not so! Something else *has* been named for me. Mr. Alex Kvassay of Wichita, Kansas, writes, "We now have a new dog. We have named him Freddy, after you."

He didn't say what kind of dog it was.

A GATHERING
AT THE RIVER

A GATHERING AT THE RIVER

The man's body was discovered in the early morning hours by a Brazilian fisherman who was gathering driftwood on a sandy beach near the point where the river empties into the Atlantic. There was no doctor nearby, but the local fishermen who were familiar with such things estimated that the corpse had been in the sea for about six hours. Sharks and the elements had done their work. The torso was severely mutilated, the face was completely destroyed. The only clothing on the body was a small piece of shirt sleeve on the left arm. There were no shoes, no jewelry, and no identifying marks.

The United States had entered World War II, and enemy submarines were increasing their activity along the coasts of South America, especially Brazil. Their prey were American merchant ships bringing supplies to new military bases, and returning to U.S. ports with bales of raw rubber and other tropical cargo. For a time these U-boats were very successful. In fact, the day before the discovery of the body, the *SS Corbis*, an American freighter returning to Baltimore from Brazilian ports, was torpedoed and sunk near the mouth of the river shortly after entering the open sea. Most of the crew were rescued, but four men were lost and presumed dead, even though a search was continuing.

Since the *Corbis* had gone down the previous day and because the mangled corpse on the beach had blond hair, there was no doubt that the dead man was an American seaman. The proper thing to do, the Brazilian fishermen reasoned, was to bring the body to the nearest American consulate in the port town several miles upriver.

After a brief shower, the tropical sun was already gathering strength for the day. Wisps of steam were curling from small potholes of muddy water in the cobblestone streets when Vice Consul Wilson arrived early that morning at his office in the American consulate. Two fishermen were already waiting for him. They informed him of the discovery and added that they had taken the dead American sailor, wrapped in a bedsheet, to the town's morgue. The morgue was an open-air shed with a red tile roof squatting in a moldy square, one block from the river. Three wooden tables covered with marble slabs stood on one side of the shed. Most of the dead brought here had died a violent death, victims of murder or homicide, and it was here that the police doctor was supposed to examine the victims. He seldom did, since the equatorial heat and a lack of refrigeration and embalming equipment made burial within a few hours after death mandatory by law.

After thanking the fishermen and giving them a small sum of money, Vice Consul Wilson duly notified the Brazilian police and the local shipping agent of the *SS Corbis*. He then went to the morgue accompanied by the town's coffin maker, who was a carpenter by trade, to examine the body. As he had expected, no officials showed up. He concluded that immediate identification was impossible and instructed the carpenter to bring a proper coffin, to place the body therein, and to leave it on one of the marble slabs. Whatever ceremony could be arranged would have to take place at the morgue as soon as possible. The carpenter, however, pointed out a slight problem. Due to rigor mortis, the right leg was bent in a rigid position at the knee to such an extent that when the body was placed in a coffin, the protruding knee would not permit the lid to close. It was finally agreed that the carpenter would simply saw a hole in the coffin top large enough to allow the knee to stick out.

A funeral service was scheduled for five p.m. at the morgue, and Miss Abigail Hawkins, the only American secretary at the consulate, was given the task of assisting Vice Consul Wilson in making the arrangements. Miss Hawkins was a prim maiden lady who numbered her years somewhere on the upside of forty. Some fifteen of those years had been spent doing missionary work in Peru and Brazil before joining the consulate staff. She was a tall, thin woman who wore her long greying hair in a neat coil on the very top of her head. The perpetual expression of belligerency on her gaunt face was the result of a lifelong losing battle against the sins of her fellow creatures. She had recently given up most of her work on behalf of the Virgin Saints of the Holy Flame—except on Sundays. The sect's headquarters in California did, however, continue to ship her large crates of religious tracts, which she distributed at every opportunity. She gave them freely to members of the American and British colony in the town as well as to the Brazilians. That the tracts were printed only in English was no deterrent, since they promised Hell's fire and damnation to sinners of every stripe—and this was also Miss Hawkins' creed.

Miss Hawkins realized that she had very little time to arrange for the funeral. Several local Brazilian priests were available, but they didn't speak English, and she had decided that the service should be conducted in English if possible. She drove in the consulate's station wagon to the nearby American air base, having in mind Padre O'Bannion, one of the base chaplains. Arriving at the base, however, she found the Padre in the last phase of one of his periodic sprees, and he was in the padded cell of the base hospital. He had recently received notice that his brother had been killed in the fighting in the Philippines, and this news had triggered his alcoholic propensity. The Padre was especially beloved at the base for his ability to transform the low grade movies at the outdoor base theater into hilarious hits. If the film was unusually bad, Padre O'Bannion would take a seat in the front row and talk back in a loud voice to the actors on the screen. The resulting dialogue, as the Padre's assistant explained to Miss Hawkins, was always much funnier than the goings-on in the movie.

"Fer instance, I remember onct," said the assistant, a lanky private from Brooklyn, as Miss Hawkins nervously consulted her watch, "we had this here pitchur with one of them new stars that nobody never heard of. Jeez! A real dog it was! Class XYZ pitchur. Well, in one place there's this babe, see? Somebody, Bell or Balls, or maybe Ball. The babe had just got herself this contract to act in Hollywood, see? But her husband, the hero, see? One of them new guys, Custer or maybe Curtis, his name was. Well, he was tellin' her he dint want her to go to no Hollywood and be breakin' up the home. This was all in the play, see? Well, the babe starts cryin' real bad. Then she waves this contract in the guy's face and says to him, 'well, whaddya want me to do with this here million-dollar contract?' And just then—right there, see, before the hero can answer back—Padre O'Bannion stands up and hollers out, 'stick it. . . . .'"

"Young man!" Miss Hawkins shouted. Her face was now flushed, and her nostrils were quivering. "I'm not at all interested in the merits of your chaplain. The plain fact is that he's a drunken sot, and the Lord will punish him! Good day, sir!"

Her next stop was at the Reverend Lunsford's small missionary church on the outskirts of the town. The Reverend was away in the interior searching for rare butterflies for his famed collection, but his organist-handyman McDougal was there sweeping the floor. McDougal was an elderly black man of unknown nationality, presumed to be a native of Trinidad who had jumped ship somewhere on the Brazilian coast. He spoke the English of the West Indies and was well known in the town for his skill at the antiquated foot-bellows organ in Reverend Lunsford's church. He had a good bass voice and also led the congregation in the hymn singing.

It was agreed that McDougal would bring the organ to the morgue and, if time permitted, he would sing a song at the funeral service.

Later that afternoon, after seeing that all was in readiness at the morgue, Vice Consul Wilson returned to the consulate to finish writing a report. About an hour before the ceremony was to begin, the Brazilian secretary informed him that he had a visitor—a fisherman from downriver who wanted to speak with him urgently.

"Very well, Miss Barros," Wilson said, "but tell him to be brief, as I have to leave right away for the funeral." The man was ushered into Wilson's office, and the secretary closed the door.

"It's about the dead American seaman, *O Senhor Consul*," the man said. He was carrying a small piece of cloth rolled into a wad. "Some children playing on the beach this morning found this only a short distance from where the body was discovered. It surely belonged to the dead American seaman, and we thought that we should bring it to you." He placed the wad of cloth on Wilson's desk, and Wilson unrolled a tattered, blood-stained piece of a man's shirt. A part of a sleeve and a button-down pocket were still intact. He immediately recognized the cloth as being of the same material as that found on the corpse.

"There is also something in the pocket, *Senhor*," the man said. "We left it there just as we found it."

Wilson unbuttoned the pocket and removed a small metal trinket. As he examined it closely, his hands trembled so that he dropped the piece on the floor, and his face turned pale. He hurriedly thanked the man, gave him a rather large sum of money, and exacted a promise that no one else would be told about this latest discovery and its delivery to the consulate. The fisherman, folding the money into his pocket, swore secrecy on the head of his mother.

Vice Consul Wilson was not what one could call a drinking man, especially not before sundown. However, after the fisherman had left, he locked his office door, took the bottle of scotch from his desk and took three long pulls directly from the bottle.

A few rows of folding metal chairs had been set up under the roof of the morgue, and the coffin was draped with the American flag, whose stripes covered the knee protruding from the hole in the lid. The organ and a lectern were in place as the hour of the funeral approached. Some of the people were already seated, the women fanning themselves with large palmetto fans and the men mopping their brows against the pervasive tropical heat.

Shortly before five p.m. Vice Consul Wilson arrived, accompanied by Miss Hawkins and McDougal. As they entered the morgue, a taxi pulled up, and the driver took from the rear seat an enormous floral arrangement of red, white and blue flowers put together in the form of the American flag. There were two or three extra stripes and a few excess stars were in the wrong places, but it was a beautiful creation, apparently done on very short notice. When the driver placed it in front of the flag-draped coffin, Miss Hawkins realized with horror that she had forgotten to order flowers. She wondered who could have sent them.

There was only a small group of Americans attending, but the consular corps was well represented by local businessmen who were honorary consuls of various countries. Among them were the local distributor of Gordon's Gin, the town's best tailor who specialized in white linen suits, the Quaker Oats importer, the leading exporter of Brazil nuts, a prominent exporter of alligator hides, and the owner of Madame Fi Fi's bordello. The local agent of the SS Corbis was there with his wife, and the Governor had sent a representative.

A crowd of the curious had gathered on the river bank near the morgue: caboclos from the interior, their black faces gleaming in the hot sun; barefooted rubber tappers off the small river boats, in their ragged trousers and open, sweaty shirts; fat native peddler women in their colorful shawls, carrying baskets of bananas and mamao fruit balanced expertly on their heads; half-dressed street urchins, carrying their shoeshine boxes—all stood and stared at the frenzied activity.

McDougal went directly to the organ and sat on the short stool. He wore his black bow tie, carefully tied around a high, stiff white collar which nearly reached his chin while leaving ample space for a prominent adam's apple. His dark suit was shiny with age and a bit frayed at the cuffs, but it was clean and newly pressed. He presented the solemn dignity of a regal monarch about to receive the homage of his loyal subjects. He had brought no music with him, but he knew from memory the tune and some of the words of the old hymn which he would sing.

The audience was seated, and Vice consul Wilson gave the signal to begin. The black man's bony hands reached slowly to the organ. Ebony fingers caressed ivory keys—so softly at first that the music was barely audible. The motley group watching from the river bank fell silent. Some of the *caboclos* removed their floppy straw hats and made the sign of the cross.

As the first bars of music were being played, three more taxis arrived. There was a gasp from the women sitting on the folding chairs. Madame Fi Fi and eight of her girls from the Red Light District got out of the taxis. All of them were dressed in black, and they walked silently to the edge of the shed, taking great care not to come under the roof. They stood together with heads bowed. The crew of the *Corbis* had been good customers. It was then that Miss Hawkins knew where the floral arrangement had come from. It was also then that she found her cheeks wet with tears.

McDougal's deep voice began, ever so softly over the subdued organ music, singing the words of an old hymn that he had learned as a child from American missionaries on some West Indian island:

> **Shall we gather at the river—**
> **The beautiful, the beautiful river?**
> **Gather with the saints at the river—**
> **That flows by the throne of God.**

He finished the hymn. The Governor's representative said a few words in praise of the brave American seaman who had given his life to keep the sea lanes open. Miss Hawkins read a few passages from her Bible and offered a short prayer for the soul of her departed fellow countryman.

The day's work around the docks was coming to a close. The light of the fading sun reflected on the *jangada* rafts on the river, coloring their sails in various shades of red. A gentle breeze from the river generously distributed the heady perfume of the sour-orange blossoms along its banks. A flock of flamingos, flying high overhead toward their roosting place on the island at the mouth of the river, caught the red glow from the west briefly on their wingtips. The aroma of roasting coffee beans mingled with the odor of rancid copra drying in the sun. It seemed a time of peace.

Vice Consul Wilson and three other men walked to the coffin to carry it the few steps to the waiting rattletrap truck which would take it directly to the cemetery. As Wilson folded the American flag and removed it from the coffin, he dropped a small white envelope through the hole in the lid. Inside the envelope was a bronze medal depicting a German U-boat surrounded by oak leaves, with the eagle and the Nazi swastika at the top—the U-boat badge issued by Hitler's Third Reich to German submarine crew members.

The gathering at the river was ended. It was one that Vice Consul Wilson would never forget.

REQUEST FOR ASYLUM

REQUEST FOR ASYLUM

At five o'clock on that crisp autumn afternoon of 1949 in Budapest, Hungary, I said goodbye to my old friend, Jeno Kovacs. I then opened the door and sent him to his death.

We were standing just inside the rear doorway of the American consulate on Victory Square and, as we shook hands for the last time, we both knew that he had only a few hours or, at best, a few days to live.

His face broke into the familiar grin that I had come to know so well over the past few years on innumerable hunting and fishing trips near his village in the hills of southern Hungary. It was a grin that usually heralded a new covey of partridge or good pheasant shooting in a winter cornfield and, afterward in the evening, a friendly glass and good talk in some small country inn.

"Never mind," he said, as he saw the anguish in my eyes. "I'm just a little guy. You did your best. But maybe one day you will do me the great favor to write about this in the newspapers in America so that people on the other side will know."

I first met Jeno shortly after I arrived in Hungary in the summer of 1945 as a consular officer. The American consulate in Budapest had just been reopened at the end of World War II. The city was in rubble; the dead from recent battles between German and Russian troops were being buried in mass graves in public parks and private gardens. The population faced a severe winter without sufficient food, fuel, or clothing. Corn and cabbage were being planted on the new graves in the center of town.

To supplement our own meager rations, another vice consul and I would drive in our jeep on weekends to farm villages and exchange a few tins of cooking fat or a few cigarettes for some fresh eggs, or, if we were lucky, a goose or a pig.

One of these trips took us to a small village near Pecs. We followed our usual procedure and parked our jeep, with an American flag on its radiator, in the village square and were soon surrounded by the curious local residents. A tall, lean young man, about twenty years old and dressed in farmer's clothing, stepped from the crowd. He clicked his heels and bowed.

"I am named Jeno Kovacs. At your service," he said, and his eyes twinkled with obvious pleasure at the opportunity to try his high-school English.

When informed of the nature of our mission to his village, he said that his father had a farm nearby with a few chickens and pigs. He added, in a conspiratorial whisper, that his father had also managed to hide a barrel of wine from the plundering Soviet troops. Would we do him the honor of accompanying him to his father's farm and perhaps to sample a glass of the wine? We would.

So began a friendship that was to last as long as he lived. I discovered that Jeno was an ardent fisherman and hunter, as was I, and I was soon spending a few weekends every month at his father's farm. We fished for trout in the summer and hunted hare, pheasant, and partridge in the autumn.

Jeno had big plans for his future. His older brother had been captured by Soviet troops and taken to Russia as a slave laborer. As soon as his brother would come home to help on the farm, he, Jeno, would set about going to the United States. There he would go directly into the U.S. Army, as this would enable him to become an American citizen earlier. Then he would study journalism and become a newspaperman. He didn't know any universities in America, but since I was from Texas, he supposed that the University of Texas was the only place to go—a supposition which I shamelessly encouraged.

By the end of 1948, the communist grip on Hungary was almost complete. The organized reign of terror and oppression by the Soviet and Hungarian political police began in earnest. All western diplomats in Budapest were constantly shadowed and harassed by police agents, and it became dangerous for Hungarians to fraternize with us.

After almost three years of hunting and fishing together, it was difficult for me to explain this danger to Jeno, but I told him that it would be better for him if I didn't visit the farm again. It was agreed that we would not meet for a while. He understood, I thought, since several people from his village had recently been herded into military trucks and taken away.

But I reckoned without Jeno's sense of justice and his desire to help his soon-to-be-adopted country. A few weeks later, he turned up in my office in Budapest and proudly placed a sheet of paper on my desk. It was a list of names of some American citizens from a nearby village who had been taken away by soldiers for slave labor in the Soviet Union. Jeno knew that the U.S. Consulate was interested in such matters.

I thanked him, then I explained carefully what could happen to him if it should be discovered by the Soviets that he was bringing information into the American consulate.

He shrugged, smiled, and said, "Never mind. I'm just a little guy. They don't notice me."

As the weeks passed and I heard nothing more from Jeno, I congratulated myself. They hadn't seen him come into the consulate. He had realized the danger. He and his family were safe.

The communist police stepped up their activities. Several prominent American and British citizens living in Hungary were arrested on false charges of spying. Two of my colleagues were declared *persona non grata* on equally false charges and ordered to leave Hungary. An American newspaper correspondent was expelled and his secretary imprisoned. Several Hungarian politicians who had opposed communism in former years were jailed, and a Hungarian clerk in the consulate was arrested and murdered in prison by the police.

The situation became so tense in Budapest that the American minister, as head of the American legation and the consulate in Hungary, held daily meetings with the staff to hear situation reports and to stress the need for extreme caution in associating with local citizens.

The expulsion of a western diplomat on charges of spying was invariably treated by the Hungarian press and radio as a great victory for communism; we Americans walked on thin-shelled eggs. But the real heroes were the Hungarian staff who continued to work at the consulate under the very real threat of death.

I was sitting at my desk in the consulate writing the final paragraph of a report when Jeno came in. It was three o'clock in the afternoon, and he had the collar of his old hunting coat turned up against the chill autumn air. He didn't say anything at first—just grinned and sat down in the chair before my desk. He was out of breath, as if he had been running. I didn't say anything either because my tongue was stuck to the roof of my mouth. I saw fear in Jeno's eyes for the first time.

"Well, I have perhaps some little troubles," he said. Before he could continue, I stepped quickly to the window of my office, which was on the second floor, and looked down into the square. A black sedan of the type used by the secret police was parked at the end of the street, and two men in raincoats and slouch hats were speaking with the uniformed Hungarian policeman who stood guard at the entrance.

"Yes. You have a little trouble. Let's hear about it quickly, because we may not have much time."

He wasted no words. A communist informer from his village had found out about the list of names which he had compiled and brought to me. His association with Americans was already well known there. The informer had reported his activities to the political police at Pecs, but a friend had warned him in time to leave home and hitch a ride into Budapest on a farm truck from a neighboring village. The police had come to the farm and, finding that he had escaped, had taken his father away.

"But never mind," he grinned. "I've made a deal with a guide who will smuggle me across the border into Austria—tomorrow night."

"Tomorrow night!" I said. "But why not tonight?"

He shook his head. "Can't. This is a professional smuggler. He makes his money by helping people escape from Hungary. He's in Austria now. Comes back here tonight, and we leave tomorrow evening as soon as it is dark. I meet him at the west terminal station of the number-twelve streetcar—tomorrow night."

I walked again to my window and peered out. The men and the sedan were gone. "Do you think the political police know that you are here?" I asked.

"I don't know, I was very careful."

In my mind, I examined the possibilities as rapidly as I could. I was about to suggest that we leave by a rear door of the consulate and go to my apartment. Then I thought of the two plain-clothed policemen who kept watch day and night outside my apartment building.

I explained to Jeno why I could not take him to my apartment to wait until the time to meet his guide. He had no other friends in Budapest and no safe place to go.

"Never mind," he said. "You will let me stay here tonight—here in the consulate. I'll leave tomorrow evening when it begins to get dark."

"Jeno," I said, "I'm going to try to do just that. I think it is your only hope. I'm going to try, do you hear? But first I have to tell the minister and get his okay. But if he says no, then I can't do it. You understand, there are certain rules—"

"But of course!" he interrupted. He was smiling again. "Of course. Ask the minister. He will say yes. This building is a part of America, no? And in America everybody is free, no? Even a little guy like me! Of course. Ask the minister."

With Jeno waiting in my office, I rushed upstairs, brushed past the minister's secretary into his office. The minister, a dour man, was considerably irritated by my interruption. I explained the situation in detail. I re-explained. I argued. Finally, I pleaded, but with no success.

"The man is not an American citizen, and even if he were, there are certain rules . . . ." The answer was no.

It was nearing closing time for the consulate, and dusk was settling over Budapest. With leaden feet and a heavier heart I made my way back to my office. Jeno was just sitting there, still smiling.

"Jeno, I'm very sorry," I began.

The smile on his face was replaced by a look of utter disbelief. "But he must not have understood! There must be some mistake! Did you explain that it is only for tonight that I am asking?"

Jeno finally understood that there was not time for an appeal of the minister's decision, and that the best I could offer him was a silent exit through an unguarded rear door. I'm afraid that he saw the tears in my eyes.

Then he shrugged. The smile returned. "Never mind," he said, "I'm just a little guy. You did your best. But maybe one day . . . ."

I opened the door and said a silent prayer.

Two weeks later, a dirty, worn envelope was left for me at the reception desk of the consulate by a shabbily dressed man who refused to give his name. It contained, in labored handwriting, a note written with pencil by Jeno's mother. It said that his body had been delivered to her by the communist police, together with an official document saying that Jeno had committed suicide while in prison. This was—and is—the usual cover for murders by the communist police. Jeno had been murdered.

So, in accordance with what was probably Jeno's last request, I set down these lines so that, as he said, "the people on the other side will know."

It's the least I can do.

WAR COMES TO NAIBA

WAR COMES TO NAIBA

Wars and other international catastrophes present a different perspective in a Brazilian jungle village than they do in London, Berlin, or New York. Nevertheless, Amazon folk will still tell you, if you have a bit of time to spare, how, on that September morning of 1939, old Schmidt, the German, and old Scarborough, the Englishman, brought World War II to their doorsteps.

It happened in the isolated village of Naiba, a typical Amazon river town. Although connected with the outside world only by the river, Naiba at one time was a flourishing little community of some two thousand souls, including the numerous rubber-tappers who spent most of their time in the interior collecting the milky sap of the *hevea brasiliensis* trees for making bales of smoked, raw rubber. Founded long ago, probably by some obscure Brazil nut exporter, Naiba had its beginning at the river's edge and gradually expanded inland, replacing a myriad of jungle trees and plants.

The town square boasted of several two-story, wooden office buildings; five bars, offering rum, beer and gin; four grocery stores and a small church built by Catholic missionaries from Sao Paulo. The church had a tiny steeple but no clock, since time, in Naiba, was never of any consequence. The rest of the square was given over to tin-covered warehouses used for storing Brazil nuts, raw rubber bales, *manioc* roots and animal hides. The few better houses, also of wood, were located some distance from the square. These houses were on higher ground and usually escaped the periodic flooding during the rainy season. A thick concrete wall, built on the outskirts of the village by the missionaries, served as a cemetery. The dead had to be interred above ground due to high water levels.

There were no town officials, with the exception of one policeman. Altercations and serious offenses, when not settled summarily with pistol, shotgun or knife by the individuals involved, were referred to the local priest for adjudication. Today, Naiba—or, rather, what is left of it—is like many of the many small Brazilian communities rotting away along the Amazon River, dreaming of past days of glory when they were boom towns.

If you'll look at those deserted, tumbled-down wooden houses, originally built on stilts near the river bank, you can see that Naiba has almost disappeared. There are probably only ten or twelve families left. They live further back there, in that jungle clearing—in those little huts with the rusting tin roofs. They make a sort of living by gathering Brazil nuts, *manioc* roots, and wild animal skins for some of the big exporting firms.

If you step around these shacks here and walk a few steps inland from the river bank, you will notice the remains of the wooden and adobe buildings and the stone church, long unused and inhabited now only by green jungle vines and a few lizards.

Take a deep breath. Smell it? It's mold. Amid the humid heat, you can smell the musty odor of the jungle. This mold attaches itself to almost everything that remains long in the Amazon—even to the people.

It is still a two-day trip by small river boat from Naiba down to Belem, the principal port at the river's mouth. The big ocean-going freighters, which go all the way up the river to Manaos, don't stop at Naiba any more. They used to, though. In fact, before World War II, two of the largest steamship lines had offices here.

Now look across the square. Can you see the front of an old wooden office building? That's it, the one covered with green mold. There's only a pile of rubble behind the facade, but you can still make out the faded sign: "HAMBURGO-GERMAN LINES." And underneath this part of the sign, if you'll look closely, are some words in small, dim letters: "Manfried Schmidt, Manager. Consular Agent of Germany." The signboard still hangs with a certain Prussian dignity above what was once a doorway.

That pile of debris over there—on the other side of the square, directly opposite the church—used to be an office of a British steamship line serving South America and Europe. Those few rotting planks are all that is left of the front of the building, but perhaps you can read part of the sign that was painted there: "BRITISH-SOOTHBY STEAMSHIP LINES." Time and its accomplices, humidity, mold and decay, have almost obscured the other words. But look down at the bottom of the sign. In small, discreet lettering: "Jas. B. Scarborough, H.B.M. Consular Agent. Manager."

James B. Scarborough and Manfried Schmidt both

arrived in the Amazon valley of Brazil as young men at about the same time. Both spent years at different posts along the river as employees of their respective shipping companies, advancing in rank as time went by. When the village of Naiba began to grow in importance as a port, British-Soothby Lines opened an office here and made Scarborough the manager. Three months later, Hamburgo-German Lines opened a similar office in the village, with Schmidt as manager, to get its share of the large shipments of Brazil nuts, hides, and bales of raw, smoked rubber destined for Europe. Schmidt was eventually appointed as a consular agent of Germany, and Scarborough became the British consular agent, thus making them both official commercial representatives of their respective countries.

Schmidt and Scarborough were the only foreigners living here. They were both bachelors, and, since the river boats stopped infrequently at the port and brought few visitors, they were inevitably drawn together after office hours to pass the time and enjoy such meager amusements as could be had in such a jungle village. Both men were fat, slightly bald, and had similar tastes. Both came from middle-class families. They had not known each other before, but in Naiba they soon became fast friends. Since Scarborough could speak no German and Schmidt spoke no English, they adopted the Portuguese of Brazil as a common language.

Scarborough had a rather large house, built of wood, just off the square on the other side of the church. It had two upstairs bedrooms and a front porch facing the river to catch any available breeze. Schmidt lived on the opposite side of the village in a similar house, except that he had no front porch.

The two friends soon developed a pattern of life to which they adhered religiously for the next twenty years. Each evening, from Monday through Friday, they would meet, after dinner, on the front porch of Scarborough's house for two games of checkers. Just two games—not more. Then, they would each drink four large bottles of Brazilian Brahma Chopp beer—just four each—while discussing the events of the day, including the latest news broadcast on Scarborough's battery-powered shortwave radio. They listened to the news primarily to get the results of the European soccer matches. After this, they would go to the village square and walk around it five times. Exactly five times—no more, no less. Then they would shake hands, say goodnight, and return to their houses.

Their program differed on Saturdays and Sundays. On Saturday afternoons, they would meet at Schmidt's house at midday for a heavy lunch. Schmidt had trained his native cook to prepare several typical German dishes which Jas. B. enjoyed even more than his host. Since their offices were closed on Saturday afternoons, after lunch they would take a long siesta in their hammocks and then go for a swim in the river.

Their Saturday evenings, including dinner, were also invariably at Schmidt's house. On these evenings, they were always entertained by two or more local maidens—an arrangement taken care of by Scarborough each Monday, a week in advance. Scarborough endeavored to have new entertainers each week but, over the years, he sometimes suspected that he was engaging in a repeat booking.

On Sundays, they always met for lunch at Scarborough's house and, after siesta, sat in the wicker chairs in front of the little bar on the square and had four gin and tonics each—exactly four—while pondering the events of the week. Punctually at seven p.m., they would leave the bar and walk around the square five times before returning to their respective houses.

For almost twenty years, until both old friends were well past sixty years of age, this routine was broken only by one or the other taking a short home-leave in Germany or in England.

Then came the third day of September 1939.

Old Jas. B. happened to turn on his shortwave set around midnight that night and heard the BBC news bulletin from London proclaiming that a state of war existed between Britain and Nazi Germany. At first he was horrified at the news. Then he became sad, and, finally, when he realized that Germany was starting another world war, a cold rage settled upon him. He decided that he must take some action to demonstrate his devotion to his country. After a few hours of fitful sleep, he went to the storeroom of his house and pulled out two very old, dusty steamer trunks. Rummaging through these, he finally found the items for which he was searching: a moth-eaten black top hat, an equally moth-eaten and rumpled formal black tailcoat, and a silver-headed walking cane. He brushed a bit of the mold from the hat and the tails, briskly polished the silver head of the cane, and waited for the dawn.

As it still does in the Amazon valley, the business day in Naiba began early to take advantage of the precious hours before the tropical heat set in. The few offices and shops around the square were already open, and the residents of the little village were just beginning their chores when Scarborough left his house that morning.

The citizens of Naiba—even those who had heard the news over Brazilian radio—were going about their daily affairs as usual. After all, how many even knew where England and Germany were located? How many cared?

They had much more important things to worry about in Naiba. They were startled, however, when O Senhor Scarborough appeared on the street and began to walk slowly across the square toward the office of the Hamburgo-German Steamship Lines. They were, in fact, so amazed that they dropped whatever they were doing and stared, for O Senhor Scarborough was wearing a black top hat and a formal tailcoat, and carried a silver-headed cane. True, the attire was a bit moldy, wrinkled, and contained not a few moth holes, but the hot morning sun glittered regally from the polished head of the cane. Indeed, Jas. B. presented a magnificent figure. No one could remember ever having seen him in such fine raiment—not even on the King's birthday! Several small boys on the street in front of the grocery shop clapped their hands and grinned in appreciation as he passed.

Scarborough made his way with great military mien to the door of this old friend's office. Schmidt was just taking some invoices and other papers from his safe. Jas. B. didn't enter the office, although the door was open, but stood just outside and rapped loudly on the side of the doorway with the silver head of his cane. Schmidt looked up from his work. Seeing Jas. B. in a resplendent costume, acting strangely, he smiled broadly and came immediately to the doorway, obviously expecting to participate in some huge new joke dreamed up by his old friend. His joyful expectations were soon completely demolished.

"Herr Consul Schmidt!" old Jas. B. roared, "again your Goddamned country has seen fit to make war on England! I inform you herewith that you and all of your Nazi swine shall go down to your dirty graves in defeat! Do you hear? Defeat! Furthermore, in the future—or what's left of it for you—I shall not speak to you again, and I'll thank you not to speak to me! And if, by chance, I see you coming toward me on the street, I'll go around you as I would a dirty, rabid dog!"

Scarborough had finished his speech before his friend realized that there was to be no joke and that the insult was in deadly earnest. Schmidt opened his mouth to say something, but, without waiting to hear, Scarborough turned on his heel, spat at his feet, and began marching away. A few yards into the square, however, Scarborough stopped and looked back over his shoulder.

Schmidt was standing in the street in front of the little office, holding his hands out toward him, palms up in supplication. Large tears were rolling off his cheeks into the dusty street. His lips were moving, apparently without sound, but they seemed to be forming in a single word, over and over, "Why? Why? Why?"

True to his word, Scarborough avoided his old friend from that time on and never spoke to him again. Two months later, the German line closed the office in Naiba and Manfried Schmidt went back to Germany.

It was about two months after Schmidt left the village that Scarborough's health began to fail. His servants began to complain to the neighbors that the old man could not sleep at night and that he spent hours speaking to himself in a strange tongue. He seemed to be all right in the office but would lose control of himself at home in the evenings. Then, shortly before Brazil declared war on Germany, a British-Soothby official stopped in Naiba one day and brought Scarborough the news that Manfried Schmidt had committed suicide in Germany.

From that day, the villagers say, *O Senhor* Scarborough's conditions grew worse, until one night he tried to hang himself on his front porch. The servants prevented him from taking his life and called the village policeman. A week later, the steamship company had the old man flown to a mental hospital in Rio de Janeiro, where he died within a few weeks.

Shortly before Scarborough died, one of the British-Soothby ship captains visited him in the Rio hospital. The captain, who had known Scarborough for many years, later said that the old man didn't recognize him and would only mumble some gibberish which was hardly understandable. The only words the captain could make out from the old man's ravings seemed completely inane. "If only I hadn't looked back," he whispered, "if only I hadn't looked . . . ."

Jas. B. was obviously crazy as a loon, the captain said.

HOLY JOE'S
TREASURE

HOLY JOE'S TREASURE

A few weeks after my arrival in Asuncion I was having lunch at the Germania, the only good restaurant in Paraguay at the time, when Elly, the Japanese waitress, placed a steaming plate of *carne asado* before me and whispered that the gentleman seated in the corner would like a word with me. "The *Senor* speaks English," she said. "I believe he is also an *Americano*." I looked at the table to which she was pointing and saw a wizened, balding, middle-aged man with a gray beard and a black eye patch.

The man walked over and pulled up a chair. "I say, mate, they told me ye're a Yank. I'm a transplanted Aussie meself. Name's Joseph Moss. Pleased t'meetcha."

So this was Holy Joe. The natives had given him the name because of his habit of reading his pocket Bible in local bars while consuming prodigious quantities of gin. He was married to a half-Indian woman and lived in a shack on

45

the outskirts of Asuncion. I already knew his story from an old-timer at the consulate. He had warned that Joe would sooner or later approach me, as he did every newcomer, with a request to finance a search for treasure. He said Joe would also produce a map showing exactly where it was buried.

According to legend, Madame Lynch—the Irish mistress of the Paraguayan, Mariscal Francisco Solano Lopez— had, in 1870 during the Triple Alliance War, hidden a trunk filled with gold somewhere in the Chaco plains of north-western Paraguay. The treasure had never been found, and Joe had spent many years searching for it.

Holy Joe had not had an easy life. In his youth, while working as a high-wire walker without a safety net in a London circus, he was partially crippled and lost his left eye when the wire broke. Out of gratitude that his life was spared, he became a missionary to South America and spent many years living among various Indian tribes in the Amazon. After contracting a severe case of malaria, he gave up missionary work and came to Paraguay, where he earned a pittance as a part-time buyer of herbs for an American company. But his real occupation, apparently, was looking for Solano's buried treasure. Whenever he succeeded in getting enough money together, he would disappear for weeks at a time, only to return empty handed and promising his backers the next trip would surely succeed.

I invited Joe to join me for coffee, but he opted for a glass of gin and immediately went into his sales pitch—complete with map. "Look, Joe," I finally said, "if Solano Lopez had any gold, it was taken out of Paraguay in 1870 by Dr. Stewart, the Scottish physician and confidant of Madame Lynch. So no treasure and no grubstake from me!"

Holy Joe was crestfallen, but only for a minute. He pocketed his map, took a hefty swig of gin, and moved his chair closer to me. He looked carefully over each shoulder. "O.K., mate, I'll give it to ye straight. I know there's no buried treasure—never was!"

I was taken aback. "But all these years you've been searching for it. Why?

"Ye see, mate, what I've been looking for is worth more than any gold Solano ever had. I've never told this to another soul before, and I'll thank ye to keep what I'm about to tell ye under yer hat. I use any money I raise, plus the little income I have, to pay for trips to the Amazon and the Matto Grosso. What I've spent half a lifetime looking for is a plant—ah, but a very special plant. Ye see, mate, the women of certain Indian tribes take a tea made from the leaves of this plant to prevent conception—a natural method of birth control. Just think of it, mate, what a fortune I could accumulate by making this available to the world!" Holy Joe's good eye beamed. "On some of my trips to the Amazon I found tribes that used it, but they're very secretive. I've brought back a few plants, but they always turned out to be the wrong ones."

"But how do you test the plants, Joe? I mean . . . ." Joe hung his head in embarrassment. He had seven children and another on the way.

I finally convinced Holy Joe that I had no money for a grubstake. But I had not seen the last of him. Over the next two years we came to be good friends. Since I shared his secret, he apparently felt obligated to come to my office after each trip, which miraculously coincided with each influx of new consular personnel, and apprise me of the results. They were always negative. I would occasionally invite him for a gin at the Lido Bar or lunch at the Germania.

During one of these lunches he confided that he felt he was getting old and his greatest fear was that he might not find the plant in time. He continued his search.

One rainy afternoon, with no urgent matters requiring attention, I stopped at the consulate reading room to look for some newspapers. I was browsing through the stack on the table when suddenly the glaring cover of an American magazine caught my eye. There it was in black and red: "The Birth Control Pill: A New Age Dawns."

With trembling hands, I hurriedly turned to the article inside. It detailed the work of a number of scientists, including Dr. Pinkus Gregory and Dr. John Rock, and stated that the new discovery was the solution to the world's population explosion. The magazine was two months old.

Holy Joe could now end his long search. I had to reach him immediately, since I knew he was about to make another trip to the Amazon. He had no telephone, so I sent a messenger to his shack with a note asking him to meet me at the Germania at six p.m. sharp. I tore the page with the article from the magazine and put it in my pocket. Since Joe read nothing except his Bible and owned no radio, I knew he would be unaware of the discovery.

He was waiting for me when I arrived. We were the only customers, since the Paraguayans dine late. Elly brought a glass of gin for Joe and beer for me. I noted at once that he was in high spirits—and he hadn't been drinking. "I've got great news, mate," he said. Before I could interrupt, he continued, "This time I've got it! This morning I met a missionary at the Sanatorio Adventista who just returned from the Matto Grosso. He gave me exact directions for reaching a small tribe there that grows the plant. Think of it! They don't search for it in the jungle like the others. They grow it near their huts! He's seen it, and he could have brought out as much as he wanted had he known anybody was interested!" Joe was euphoric. I was reaching into my pocket for the magazine article when he added, "Ye know, mate, this is the happiest day of my life. I'm going to be rich. I'm setting off for the Matto Grosso for the last time end of this week."

I slowly withdrew my hand from my pocket—without the magazine article. I excused myself and went to the toilet, where I tore the article into tiny shreds and flushed it down.

"By the way, mate, what did ye want to see me about? I mean, the note," Joe said when I returned to the table.

I finished my beer in one gulp. "Well, er, actually I knew you'd be leaving on another trip soon, and uh, well, I just happen to have a little spare cash. Not much, you know, and I thought maybe . . . ."

THE
MILLION-
DOLLAR
BUSINESS

THE MILLION-DOLLAR BUSINESS

The plan began with a letter to the American consulate in Rangoon, Burma, from the Heavenly Tidings Mission, a religious organization in California. It was signed by Miss Pricilla Whitberry, Director, and stated that in the interest of helping the poor people of Burma and also to generate some funds to further the Mission's good works, they were prepared to import a considerable quantity of Burmese handicraft. In addition to wholesaling the merchandise to souvenir shops throughout the United States, the Mission would offer them for sale at their various temples in California. Miss Whitberry was particularly interested in wood-carvings of elephants, statuettes of native dancers, gilded lacquerware sewing boxes and bon-bon containers made in the form of ducks. She was quite enthusiastic and estimated that she could sell a million dollars worth of Burmese handicraft per year. She ended her letter with the notice that she would soon arrive in Rangoon to inspect potential purchases and to place firm orders with exporters recommended by the consulate.

The letter was forwarded by the consulate to the Burmese Ministry of Industry and Commerce, where I was serving temporarily as an adviser on trade promotion. The Minister summoned me to his office.

"I've talked this over with the General, himself," the Minister said, indicating Miss Whitberry's letter. "This is a million-dollar business! The General believes that this would be an excellent opportunity to persuade some of the villages around Pagan and Mandalay to stop making opium pipes and selling drugs for those Golden Triangle gangsters. We have to convince them that they can earn more by making these things for sale in America. It will not be easy. They have been making opium pipes up there for centuries."

The result of this conversation was that my Burmese assistant, U. Saw Myint, and I would receive Miss Whitberry upon her arrival at Mingaladon airport and bring her to her hotel. After a night's rest, we would show her around Rangoon and Kemmendine, where Burmese parasols and textiles are made. We would then travel with her to a principal lacquerware and woodcarving village near Pagan, an ancient Buddhist temple town on the Irrawaddy River. Miss Whitberry could indicate the items in which she was interested and later place her order with an export firm in Rangoon.

U. Saw, my assistant, was a young man whose main interests in life were eating and cockfighting, in that order. In the office, he ate a bowl of rice mixed with an evil-smelling fish sauce every hour and spent the rest of his time on the telephone buying or selling fighting cocks. He was assigned to me by the Minister because of his supposed knowledge of English. Actually, he spoke very little English. With him as my interpreter, I contemplated Miss Whitberry's travels in Burma with some apprehension.

We met Miss Whitberry at the airport on schedule. She was a stout maiden lady, well beyond middle age, of stern visage and military mien. Her gray hair, which she wore in a bun, was covered by a wide-brimmed, floppy straw hat. She came off the plane carrying a huge canvas handbag in one hand and a Bible in the other. One sensed immediately that Miss Whitberry was a no-nonsense person.

I had left the hotel arrangements to U. Saw, assuming that he would make a reservation for Miss Whitberry at the Strand, Rangoon's tourist hotel. I was astonished to find that he had booked her into a small inn, of which I had never heard, in Paradise Valley on the outskirts of the city.

Miss Whitberry was the only guest at the inn, but the Chinese room clerk, who was sleeping behind his desk when we arrived, assured us that the room was first class. There was no dining room, but meals and tea would be served in the room. We wished Miss Whitberry a pleasant night and agreed to return for her early the next morning.

U. Saw was just finishing his first bowl of the day of malodorous rice when Miss Whitberry came into the office at the ministry. Her face was drawn, there were dark rings under her eyes, and the floppy hat was askew. She was carrying her canvas handbag and her Bible. She was visibly upset.

"We were just about to leave for your hotel," I assured her, although it was quite early. "Have you had your breakfast?"

Miss Whitberry stared at us out of bloodshot eyes, as U. Saw gulped the last stinking bite from his rice bowl. "No, I can't eat. I have a taxi waiting with my luggage," she said wearily. "I've asked him to take me to another hotel. Perhaps you can come and give him directions. I didn't sleep a wink last night! Actually the room was quite nice. The bed was extra large and comfortable and even had a pink silk cover. I was especially impressed with the mirrors—why there was even a beautiful, large mirror on the ceiling right above the bed and the most extraordinary gadgets in the bathroom. I wondered what on earth they are for!"

I looked at U. Saw. He quickly busied himself with some papers.

"But there was some sort of party in the hotel," she continued. "I've really never heard such noises in my life! Men shouting. Women laughing and screaming. It went on the whole night. Of course, I couldn't understand what they were saying. I wanted to get the manager, but I was afraid to leave my room."

En route to the Strand Hotel with Miss Whitberry, I tried to offer some explanation for the inconvenience. "You see, the inn in Paradise Valley is actually a businessman's hotel. I'm sure that U. Saw didn't think of that when he booked you in there. You know the Burmese conduct much of their business at night, the days here being so warm, and, of course, they can be quite noisy in some of their bargaining."

Miss Whitberry agreed that it was certainly an unusual way to do business and was greatly relieved when I assured her that she would be able to make all of her purchases during the daytime. We postponed the Rangoon tour until the following day.

I returned to the office to find a repentant U. Saw who swore on the head of Buddha that he hadn't known that the Paradise Valley Inn was a bordello, even though it was owned by his cousin.

A few days later, Miss Whitberry, U. Saw, and I disembarked at Pagan from the ancient paddle wheel steamer, which had once seen service on the Mississippi River. A Burmese army officer in Pagan provided a topless jeep, and, after a nerve-wracking, dusty drive with U. Saw at the wheel, we arrived just before noon at the lacquerware village. Official notice of our visit had been sent, and we were met by the headman, who was introduced by U. Saw as Mr. Nouk, and four of his assistants.

Mr. Nouk was a short man of indeterminate age with a belly resembling a fat Buddha. The top of his enormous head was swathed in a pink silk kerchief, a part of which dangled over his right ear. In spite of the hot weather, he wore the traditional, black, cotton-cloth, long sleeved jacket over his white shirt. A checked *longyi* wrap-around skirt reached his sandal-clad feet. A cartridge belt around his waist held a .45 caliber semi-automatic pistol. Flanked by his four similarly-clad assistants, Mr. Nouk gave us a Halloween-pumpkin smile, revealing stained, stubby teeth.

"How do you!" he said, and this appeared to be the extent of his English, as it was followed by a long statement in Burmese while Miss Whitberry, U. Saw, and I stood more or less at attention surrounded by a cluster of scrawny chickens and naked children.

"He say," U. Saw translated, "you, me and old lady from America most welcome to village. He say we sleep tonight in guest house, and he have made special lunch our honor. After, he show old lady lacquerware and woodcarving."

The lunch was served in the dining hall of the guest house, which was a typical, large, wooden house on stilts, in the middle of the village. Mr. Nouk and his four assistants sat on one side of the table facing Miss Whitberry, who was the only female present, U. Saw and myself. The food was a heavily spiced, boiled meat, served with rice. The beverage was scotch whiskey, and tea. Miss Whitberry immediately asked for water, and a servant brought her a glass of brown liquid, which I advised her not to drink. She opted for tea. When Mr. Nouk began the conversation with a question to Miss Whitberry, I distinctly heard the words, "America" and "John Wayne."

"He say," U. Saw interpreted, "old lady come from America. She know John Wayne."

"John Wayne! Good boy!" Mr. Nouk shouted, jumping to his feet and cradling an imaginary machine gun in his arms. "Rat-ta-ta-ta-ta-tat!" This was followed by a stream of Burmese.

"He say like John Wayne very much. See him five time in movie house Mandalay. He say he prepare nice gift for John Wayne—half pound best grade A-one opium and beautiful opium pipe. Old lady take with and give John Wayne in America—from good friend, U. Nouk."

The color drained from Miss Whitberry's face. "Oh! Good Heavens, no! Tell him please that I don't know Mr. Wayne at all. Opium is a drug, isn't it? Goodness no! I could never do that!"

Mr. Nouk was extremely disappointed and inquired of U. Saw if he was certain that Miss Whitberry was an American.

Miss Whitberry recovered her composure and finished the extra large portion of food on her plate. "Tell Mr. Nouk," she said, "this is the most delicious meal I've ever eaten. Ask him, please, what kind of meat it is."

U. Saw duly communicated this to Mr. Nouk who beamed with pleasure. His answer, however, brought a puzzled expression to U. Saw's face. He thought for a moment then took out his small Burmese-English dictionary and thumbed through the pages. "Aha! Yes. He say it what you call in English the mole. It meat of the mole. He cook it specially your honor!"

Miss Whitberry quickly excused herself and went to the toilet. I took an extra large swallow of Scotch.

The first hut that we visited after lunch contained five workmen busily making opium pipes. Mr. Nouk explained the process, without mentioning the opium, and added that he was certain that these would sell extremely well in America.

"Heavens no!" Miss Whitberry said. "Tell him that our Mission would never consider anything that would promote the use of tobacco. We consider the use of tobacco to be a sin."

The rest of the afternoon was spent inspecting other workshops, and Miss Whitberry was pleased to find some lacquerware items and woodcarvings to add to her import list. Mr. Nouk and two of his assistants joined us in the guest house for the evening meal, which was canned salmon and rice. Miss Whitberry insisted on watching the cook open the cans. As we were about to leave the table, Mr. Nouk flashed his pumpkin smile and directed a question to me.

"He say how many girl you want tonight."

"Tell him," I said, "that I thank him for his thoughtfulness, but it has been a long day. We are rather tired, and we must get up early to catch the steamer in Pagan. Perhaps another time."

A frown and another stream of rapid Burmese from Mr. Nouk.

"He say he supply many nice girl to brave English soldier during war." U. Saw added an aside, "He also supply many nice girl to brave Japanese soldier during war."

My attempt at a second refusal was interrupted by another burst from Mr. Nouk.

"He say Ho Kay! Ho Kay! You want sleep with old American lady, that your business!"

Miss Whitberry fled to her room with her hands cupped over her ears.

The next morning, as we prepared to depart for Pagan, Mr. Nouk and two of his sides came to see us off. After a long speech thanking us for the visit, he directed a question to me. Again, I caught the words "John Wayne" and "America."

"He say maybe you give him John Wayne address in America."

Not wishing to be considered by Mr. Nouk as un-American, I said that I was sorry but that I had left Mr. Wayne's address in my office in Rangoon. He seemed to be satisfied with this explanation. As the jeep took off in a cloud of dust, I looked back and saw Mr. Nouk again waving his imaginary machine gun and heard him shouting, "John Wayne! Good Boy! Rat-ta-ta-ta-ta-tat!"

Miss Whitberry placed a firm order with a Chinese exporter in Rangoon for several hundred dollars worth of lacquerware, parasols, and woodcarvings. At the airport, U. Saw and I had the impression that she was happy to be leaving. The Minister complimented us for a job well done.

One day, several months later, the commercial officer from the American Embassy in Rangoon charged into my office. I suspected immediately that something unusual was afoot, since we rarely had a visitor of his rank from the Embassy. He was in a foul mood.

"Just what the Hell are you guys doing over here?" he shouted, pounding my desk with his fist.

U. Saw choked on a mouthful of rotten fish sauce and rice, and before I could ask what the trouble was, the commercial officer tossed a letter on my desk.

"Look at this! You trying to create an international scandal or something? You guys ought to be put in jail!"

The letter, addressed to the American Ambassador, Rangoon, was on the stationery of the Heavenly Tidings Mission.

Dear Sir:

I am writing you about a most dreadful situation. There are some men here from Washington, D. C. who want to send Reverend McPhearson, our president, and me to prison.

You will recall that sometime ago the Mission ordered a quantity of Burmese handicraft items from an exporter recommended by the Ministry of Industry and Commerce in Rangoon. Imagine! When the customs people here opened some of the crates, they found only those little pipes which they say are for smoking drugs! But worst of all, the rest of the boxes contained the most horrible woodcarvings—which they say are pornographic material!

The men from Washington think that our only salvation would be an official letter from the ministry and one from the consulate stating that I did not order any of these horrid things.

Please do send these letters immediately.

Yours,
Ms. Pricilla Whitberry, Director.

We sent the letters, wished Miss Whitberry good luck and said good-bye to the million-dollar business.

A few days later, the telephone rang. It was the American consul's secretary. "We are wondering," she said, "if you by any chance have the address of John Wayne, the film star?

We have this funny little man here at the consulate. He's a big fan of John Wayne movies and has brought along this gift package which he wants us to mail to Mr. Wayne. He says you have Mr. Wayne's address."

In a tremulous voice I asked her if she knew what was in the package.

"Oh, yes! It's the cutest little Burmese pipe, decorated with ribbons, and a half-pound of a very expensive, very special type of Burmese tobacco. We think it will be a very nice gesture from a Burmese citizen. Now, if you'll just . . . ."

RENDEZVOUS
AT
TOMASELLI'S

RENDEZVOUS
AT TOMASELLI'S

I hadn't seen nor heard from Henderson for some thirty
years. Consequently, I was surprised when his letter from
San Francisco reached me at the small farming village in the
Black Forest of Germany, where I lived in retirement. His
letter recalled our tour of service together in Salzburg,
Austria shortly after World War II and inquired if I would
accompany him to Salzburg in the coming spring. Since he
mentioned that he, too, was retired, I assumed that his
proposed trip would be merely a sentimental journey to
rekindle old war memories. I was, however, puzzled by a
line in his letter saying that he would have to be in Salzburg
on the next twenty-sixth of May. Other than mentioning
that he had my address from a mutual friend and that he
would be traveling alone, he gave no details of his life since
our days together in Austria.

After a brief exchange of letters, it was agreed that Henderson would spend a week in May as my house guest, after which we would drive in my car to Salzburg to be there on May twenty-sixth. I would use the occasion for a long overdue visit with my cousin who lived there, and Henderson would either continue by train to Vienna or fly back to San Francisco from Munich. His letters were rather vague as to his plans after Salzburg.

I had met Henderson during my first week in Salzburg, shortly after World War II. The town was in the American-occupied zone of post-war Europe, and he was stationed there as a lieutenant in the U.S. Army. He had something or other to do with military intelligence. I worked in the American consulate. We both had rooms in Parsch, where each weekday morning we would board the dinky narrow-gauge train to commute to our respective offices in the center of town—he to a desk in the police station and I to the consular offices. We were both bachelors of about the same age, and we soon became fast friends.

The U.S. Army had requisitioned practically all of the hotels, restaurants and coffee houses in Salzburg, but Americans were permitted to bring Austrian guests for a meal, a drink or a coffee. Henderson's blond good looks insured his instant success with the local Austrian ladies, and he usually had several of them as lunch or dinner guests. His favorite, however, was a stunningly beautiful blonde named Johanna. She had the bluest eyes that I've ever seen. Johanna soon became Henderson's steady companion, and they could usually be seen evenings at Tomaselli's, the old baroque coffee house on *Alte Markt* square in the heart of Salzburg. I would sometimes join them there—always at the same table—after office hours for a coffee, brandy and lively conversation.

One of the curses of foreign service life is the fleeting nature of friendships. Good friends are together for a few months or for two or three years, then they are suddenly separated by assignments to other countries, sometimes half a world away. So it was that after about a year in Salzburg I received orders to go to Singapore. I said goodby to my friends, including Henderson. I was not to see him again for over thirty years.

Henderson arrived on schedule in May and took a taxi from the village railway station up to my villa. It was good that he did so, since I would not have recognized him in a crowd—just as it is probable that he would not have known me.

I greeted an elderly, baldheaded, paunchy man. The fringe of hair which nature had left him was completely white, and the lines on his tanned face were deep. Time had obviously not treated him with an abundance of kindness, and it took a while before a vague caricature of the old Henderson I had known in Salzburg began to emerge. We sat on my terrace with gin tonics and talked deep into the balmy night, reminiscing as old men do, and planning our trip to Austria. I finally asked him why he had to be in Salzburg exactly on the twenty-sixth of May.

He was silent for a while, and I began to think that he did not intend to answer. "When you were young," he finally said, "did you ever say to yourself—or to someone else— 'someday, when I am old, I would like to come here to this place, exactly this spot, and recreate this very moment to prove that it will never be lost in time?'"

I admitted that, given my lack of imagination, the thought had never occurred to me.

"It happened to me once—in Salzburg," Henderson continued. "I couldn't say whether it was a result of the place, the special event, the particular time or the unusual person who was there with me. Maybe I was influenced by all of these, but it did happen to me. Do you remember Johanna? She and I always had the same table every evening at Tomaselli's—the first table on the left as you enter from *Alte Markt* square. That table was always reserved for us."

I did, indeed, remember. I also recalled Johanna's regal bearing and her incredible beauty.

"It was on the evening of my thirty-first birthday, May the twenty-sixth," Henderson said. "That was shortly after you had left Salzburg. Johanna and I were sitting at our usual table at Tomaselli's having coffee and brandy after a memorable birthday dinner. It had been a wonderful day, and we were both in high spirits. She had made a new dress for herself out of some material which she had scrounged, and I had brought her a scarf which matched her blue eyes. She was more beautiful that evening than ever! Suddenly, only half in jest, I said to her, 'let's come here—to this very table—on my sixty-fifth birthday.' We both laughed heartily, and then she said, 'no, you will retire only at sixty-five. Let's make it on your sixty-sixth birthday—and we'll be too old to come late in the evening. We'll come for tea at five o'clock in the afternoon,' and with a mischievous glint in her eyes, she added, 'and to make sure that we recognize each other, we will each bring two roses, a red one and a yellow one.' I agreed, and we gleefully raised our glasses.

I suppose that both Johanna and I were thinking that one day I would ask her to marry me. However, I knew that I would soon be transferred back to the States, and I didn't want to stay in the army. I decided that I would look for a job in private industry in California and then propose marriage to her. Unfortunately, I also decided that it would be best not to discuss my plans with her until I had found a suitable job.

About a month after my birthday celebration at Tomaselli's, I was ordered back to Washington, D.C. I took a train to go to the airport in Frankfurt, Germany. Johanna came with me to the railway station in Salzburg. We both cried, and I said that I'd see her soon. She ran alongside my window of the moving train as far as she could, waving her scarf. It was the last time I saw her.

I got out of the army and found a job in California. Johanna and I corresponded regularly at first, telling each other little everyday things. she had found a job as a secretary in Salzburg. I was made assistant chief of a sales department. She had acquired a cat. I had bought some goldfish.

That first year I kept thinking each month that I would ask Johanna to join me, but there was always a question of money. My salary was small, so I would have to wait for a promotion. After the second year, and no promotion, our letters to each other lessened considerably, and their contents became more stilted. By the end of the third year our letters ceased, except for the birthday cards. I received a card from Johanna on my birthday every year for six or seven years. They, too, finally stopped, but I remember that the last birthday card contained a note saying, 'see you at Tomaselli's.' I knew what she meant.

I eventually married—a lovely girl who worked in the office with me. I started my own company, which was quite successful. We had a son, who is head of the company now that I have retired. Unfortunately, my wife died of cancer three years ago."

"And do you really believe," I asked, "that next week on May twenty-sixth—assuming that Johanna is still alive and still in Salzburg—that she will remember that it is your sixty-sixth birthday and that she will be in Tomaselli's coffee house at five p.m.?"

Henderson was deep in his thoughts for a while before he replied. "No. Not really. I guess that would be too much to expect, even if she is alive. It was too long ago. I suppose that all I'm trying to do is to relive a part of my youth in a place where I enjoyed some of my happiest moments."

By getting an early start on the morning of May twenty-sixth, Henderson and I drove into Salzburg shortly before noon. It was a beautiful spring day, and the town was beginning to fill with pre-season tourists. I drove directly to *Getreidegasse* and the *Goldener Hirsch* hotel, where Henderson had booked a room. I left him and his bags there and drove to my cousin's house in Anif, a village near Salzburg, where I was to have lunch and spend the night.

I met Henderson at the hotel after lunch, and we set out on foot to explore our old haunts. I had been in Salzburg several times since our post-war days, but it was Henderson's first visit since he was there in the army. We walked to Parsch, on the other side of the river, and he was constantly amazed by the changes. The dinky railway was gone. The Displaced Persons camp had given way to huge apartment buildings. The house where we once had rooms was now a handworkers' school. Eder's hotel no longer existed; in its place was a shiny, modern bank.

From Parsch we walked down to the railway station, pausing here and there to point out a familiar landmark. The old cobblestone streets were crowded with people in shirt sleeves and light dresses. The majestic, horse-drawn carriages were doing a brisk business with groups of wide-eyed tourists. Henderson's conversation was animated and, although we hadn't talked further about five o'clock tea, I could see that he was under a nervous strain. He looked at his watch frequently and finally said that perhaps we had best make our way back toward Tomaselli's. We wanted to be there well before five o'clock.

We stopped at the flower stall in the railway station, and Henderson bought two beautiful roses, one red and one yellow. He asked the salesgirl to tie them together with a blue ribbon. This caused some confusion, but she finally found a piece of ribbon and made a lovely bow, which cost twenty schillings extra.

It was half past four p.m. when we walked into Tomaselli's through the *Alte Markt* entrance. Henderson immediately remarked that everything was the same as when he was last there—the somber waiters in their black, shiny suits, white shirts, black bow ties and black shoes of worn but highly polished leather; the marble-topped tables and uncomfortable, straight-backed chairs; the racks containing newspapers attached to wooden sticks; the circular *pissoir* in the back and the long sideboard containing such culinary delights as *dobos torte*, *Linzer torte*, apple strudel, rum, chocolate and cheese cakes and many others. Indeed, Tomaselli's had survived much worse calamities than the American occupation. It had been dispensing coffee and sweets in Salzburg since 1764.

We were in luck. The afternoon tea crowd had not yet arrived. There were a few German hippies with back packs sitting in the front of the room near the *Alte Markt* entrance, and a cluster of elderly English tourists, including a bearded man with one arm and a woman in a wheelchair, chatting away over tea and cake in the back of the room. The Austrian aristocracy was represented by two gentlemen with beards and knee breeches and an elegantly dressed old lady wearing dark sunglasses and with her gray hair arranged in a neat coiffure. She was addressed by the waiters as "*Gräfin*." She seemed to monopolize the conversation at her table but showed no interest in us.

We went directly to Henderson's old table, which was unoccupied, and he took a chair which would allow him a view of the entire room and both doorways. After looking around the room carefully, he made a big show of placing the roses in the exact center of the table. No one hurries at Tomaselli's, so while we waited for a waiter, we scrutinized each face in the room.

"It's really no good," Henderson said. "I know I wouldn't recognize her. We can only rely on the roses. If she comes, she'll see them; she knows the table." I agreed and waved again for a waiter. We ordered two coffees, at outrageously high prices, and Henderson mentioned to the waiter the names of several people who had worked at Tomaselli's in the old days. The waiter shook his head slowly. Sorry.

Shortly after five o'clock all of the tables were occupied. Many people spend an entire afternoon in an Austrian coffee house with a cup of coffee and a newspaper, and I noticed that only a few of the patrons who were there when we arrived had left. Many of them were probably there for the entire afternoon. The "*Grafin*" was on her third cup of coffee and once, out of the corner of my eye, I saw her staring at the roses on our table.

It was almost six o'clock, and I sensed that Henderson was resigned to the fact that Johanna would not come. We talked of old times, and he showed me pictures of his family and his home in San Francisco. I was about to suggest that we leave when suddenly a well dressed, elderly Austrian lady approached our table. She looked for a moment at the roses. "Excuse me," she said in German, "is this seat free?" She indicated the empty third chair at our table.

We both stared at her for a few seconds before Henderson shook his head sadly. "I'm sorry," he said, "we are waiting for someone." Her eyes were brown.

We switched from coffee to brandy and sat for another hour. The crowd finally began to dwindle. "Well, that's it,"

Henderson said with a wistful smile. "Of course, I really didn't expect her." I nodded agreement.

We paid our bill. Henderson left the two roses, tied with their blue ribbon, on the table, and we walked back to the *Goldener Hirsch* hotel. We sat for a while in the small lobby, which was almost too narrow for the many deer horns decorating the walls, and had two more drinks. Henderson said that he would take the train the next morning for Vienna, spend a few days there and then fly back to San Francisco. I would spend the night at my cousin's house and drive back to the Black Forest after breakfast. We said our goodbyes, promised to write, shook hands and I started walking down *Getreidegasse* to pick up my car in the parking lot. The day was ending, and the streets were filled with home-goers from shops and offices. The entire street was given over to pedestrians, many licking ice cream cones while they window shopped.

I was crossing the street in front of Mozart's birthplace on *Getreidegasse* when I saw her. She was sitting in a wheelchair, attempting to look into a shop window. I recognized her immediately as the gray-haired woman in the wheelchair who had been with the English group at Tomaselli's. The first thing that caught my attention, however, was the young girl who was pushing the wheelchair. She was probably in her early twenties and had long blonde hair and blue eyes. For a moment my thoughts raced back through the years, and I could clearly picture her sitting, laughing at Henderson's table at Tomaselli's. They didn't notice me when I stopped and pretended to look into a neighboring shopwindow. The old woman had her legs partially covered with a light blanket, but I could see that both ankles were tightly bandaged. Apparently a stroke had left the right side of her body paralyzed, and she seemed to have no control of her facial muscles. Her head was held upright by a metal brace, but her white hair was beautifully combed, and the blue eyes had not lost their sparkle. As I turned and hurried past the wheelchair, I saw the roses—one red and one yellow, tied with a pretty blue ribbon. She carried them in her lap, pressed awkwardly between two horribly twisted hands.

I never told Henderson that Johanna had kept her rendezvous at Tomaselli's. I don't think she would have wanted it that way.

SIMON McDOUGAL— IN JAIL

SIMON McDOUGAL—IN JAIL

Something in the back of my mind warned me not to open the envelope. But there were other considerations: Consul McLaughlin himself had placed it on my desk, and after all it was my first post in the Foreign Service. Belem do Para, Brazil was the post and, as my beautifully engraved visiting cards proclaimed, I was a vice consul of the United States of America. What this actually meant was that the buck stopped with me—on its way down.

The envelope was dirty and grease-stained. It had been left with the night watchman at the consulate. It was addressed, with pencil in an unsteady hand, to "Consul Sir, USA." On the back was written, "From Simon Bolivar McDougal—in Jail."

I opened it. The message therein, scrawled on a piece of brown paper bag, was brief and to the point. "Consul, Sir. I be American Citizen. I be in jail and not my fault. You please, sir, come remove me this place."

I checked the consular records of Americans residing in the consular district and found nothing regarding McDougal. What to do? As with most things in life, there were at least two possibilities: I could throw the letter into the trash, thereby risking the wrath of some vote-hungry congressman should it later be found that the man was an American, or I could go down to the local jail and talk to Mr. McDougal. Bearing in mind what I had been told in Washington about congressmen in general, I opted for the latter.

It was 1943, and Brazil was preparing to send troops to fight with the allies in World War II. Consequently, I found the chief of police to be very pro-American. The chief told me that Mr. McDougal was a frequent inmate of his jail and that he had probably been in the Amazon for some fifteen or twenty years. His nationality was unknown. He had no personal documents but was presumed to be a native of Trinidad who had jumped ship in Belem. He was not really a criminal, the chief assured me, but was considerably addicted to *cachaca*, the local rum. It seems that, when in his cups, Mr. McDougal would position himself at the intersection of two of the busiest streets in town and begin preaching a sermon while standing on a wooden box. It was one of these sermons which had led to his latest incarceration.

"Of course, you will appreciate," said the chief, "that we really can't permit such conduct, even though *O Senhor* McDougal usually gives a part of his sermon in English, which, naturally, the people on the street cannot understand. He also creates a traffic hazard."

A policeman took me to a corner cell for an interview with Mr. McDougal, who was reclining on a straw mattress, obviously recovering from a monumental binge. He was a lean, middle-aged black man, dressed only in a pair of patched trousers. He wore no shirt and no shoes, which was not unusual for laborers in the tropical heat of Belem. He was fluent in Portuguese and spoke the English of the West Indian islands, but understanding him in either of these languages was made difficult by the absence of his two upper front teeth.

McDougal, who saluted and insisted on standing at attention when he heard that I was from the consulate, confirmed that he had no personal documents and no proof of American citizenship. He said that his mother, before her death back in Trinidad, had told him that he was a U.S. citizen. He had never been to the United States; he didn't know where his parents were born and had no living relations that he knew of and no family members in Brazil.

He had never known his father. He worked sometimes, he said, on the docks in Belem unloading cargo from the river boats. As a child in Trinidad, he had worked as a house boy for a family of American missionaries. They had taught him to play the organ, and now he sometimes earned a few *cruzeiros* playing on Sundays at the Reverend Lunsford's small missionary church in Belem. He had also worked for a time as a sweeper in the bordello of Madame Ze Ze in the Red Light District, but he was fired when the madame caught him stealing the raw onions the girls kept behind their curtains to ward off disease.

"Consul, sah, you remove me this jail and get me USA passport, and I going to USA and get me fine job. Make lots money!"

After making it clear, or so I thought, to McDougal that I really couldn't help him unless we could document his claim to American citizenship, I slipped him a few *cruzeiros*, returned to the consulate, and wrote the State Department to check further into his citizenship claim.

Although I realized that there was a very slim chance that he was an American citizen, his sorrowful plight and snaggle-toothed grin aroused my youthful sympathy. Since he said that he had worked for the Reverend Lunsford, I decided to visit the minister, whom I had previously met at the consulate, and make further inquiries.

The Reverend Lunsford, an elderly Protestant missionary, had been in the Amazon valley for about thirty years and had built with his own hands the small church on the outskirts of Belem. The tiny church seated about 25 people—quite ample for his regular Sunday service, which was usually given before some twelve or fifteen people. His flock included the family of the British manager of the local power plant, the family of the importer of a famous British gin, and a few American residents. On occasion, some members of the British and American consulates were also present. I found Reverend Lunsford in his church making some repairs to this antiquated foot-bellows organ, which stood on a small platform in the corner behind his pulpit.

"Ah yes. Poor McDougal," the minister said, shaking his head sadly. "The best organist I ever had. Didn't read music, of course, but he knew all of the old hymns, and he was very good with the sound effects which I use in most of my sermons."

McDougal was especially effective on certain occasions when he had imbibed a bit too liberally from the bottle of *cachaca* which he kept hidden somewhere in the innards of the organ. The reverend knew about the bottle, and McDougal was aware that he knew. But, according to the minister, it was a delicate subject which was never discussed between them, and McDougal was very careful never to be seen drinking or depositing a fresh bottle in the instrument. Reverend Lunsford, although thoroughly disapproving of strong drink, had, over the span of years, decided that in McDougal's case a few drops did perhaps improve the sound effects.

"But, alas," the reverend said, almost in tears and wringing his hands, "a most dreadful thing happened last Easter Sunday in the church, and I had to dismiss the poor chap. It almost broke my heart, since he had been with me for many years."

On that fateful holiday, every seat in the church was filled. "It was the best attendance we'd had all year, praise the Lord, and some of the town's greatest sinners were there," the reverend said. The sermon was to be longer than usual. The missionary was in good voice. The pedals were oiled, and McDougal was at his place behind the organ.

All went well through the initial hymn singing, and Reverend Lunsford launched into his sermon. He soon reached the passage which called for the sound effects. He raised his eyes heavenward and shouted in stentorian tones: "And I heard a voice from heaven, as the voice of a great thunder . . . ." Here he raised both arms high into the air, which was McDougal's cue to work the organ bellows forcefully with both feet and to pounce on the bass notes to rattle the church walls with thunder.

But from McDougal's corner came not a sound.

The reverend paused, arms still raised to the heavens, and peered anxiously over his shoulder at the organ. Still no sound. He repeated the passage, louder this time, and frantically pumped both arms in the air while glaring at the organ. There was a deathly silence. Then suddenly from behind the organ came a very loud belch, followed immediately by a fervent "Amen" from the same source.

"Naturally, I could not possibly keep the poor fellow in the job after such a humiliating performance," the reverend said.

Two days later, McDougal came to see me in the consulate. The police chief had, in deference to my visit, released him—I later learned that he had told the chief that I had promised him a job. He stood at attention before my desk and saluted. He was still dressed in his patched trousers, but this time he was wearing a pajama top and one shoe. He explained that according to the new decree issued by Governor Barata, no one could ride the local trolley cars without wearing a jacket and shoes. The pajama top qualified as a jacket, and since the decree failed to specify *how many* shoes, the shoe, which he had borrowed for the day from a friend, placed him safely within the limits of the law. The pajama top, he claimed, was his own.

"Consul, sah, you know I be American. You be American. So I think maybe you help me find good job until my passport, she come from America. Maybe, consul, sah, you also lend me ten dollah. I pay back soon I get good job."

Truth to tell, I didn't have ten dollars, but I gave him a few more *cruzeiros* and promised to speak with an exporter friend about a job. As it so happened, my friend, Jose Levy, did have work for him, and in a few days McDougal was unloading hides on the docks. I congratulated myself on a deed well done.

At the end of the month I went down to the docks to get some information for a report to the department regarding raw rubber shipments. It was nearing noon as I was walking back to the consulate through the center of town, when I saw a small crowd gathered at the intersection of two of the busiest streets. As I neared the perimeter of the gathering, I suddenly heard a shout in English, "And the Lawd, he say, 'Adam?' Adam, he say, 'Sah!'" Two days later, I found another grimy envelope on my desk. On the back was written, "From Simon Bolivar McDougal—in Jail."

If the gods were not smiling on me that day, at least they were not frowning, because this time I did not have to visit the jail. The police chief telephoned me and offered to release McDougal if I would simply *try* to find him a job—preferably as far away from Belem as possible. The chief tried to make the offer sound like a great favor on his part, but I heard a distinct sigh of supreme happiness when, like a fool, I agreed.

McDougal stood at rigid attention before my desk and saluted. "Consul, sah, that job on docks, she no good for me. You please speak to Reverend Lunsford that he take me back full time. I not take rum anymore. I learned me lesson now."

So it came to pass that McDougal, through my intervention, was again employed by the minister. He had promised on the grave of his dead mother to forgo the demon rum. He was not only to play the organ on Sundays in Belem but also to accompany the reverend on his missionary trips up the Amazon. The minister agreed that it would be un-Christian of him, praise the Lord, not to give the poor chap another chance. Besides, McDougal was the best organist in the area.

The State Department finally replied that McDougal was not a citizen and therefore not entitled to the protection of the U.S. government. I didn't bother to inform him of the bad news immediately. He had been back working for Lunsford for two months, and I again congratulated myself that all was going well.

Shortly thereafter, on a Monday morning, I arrived at the consulate to begin my daily routine. I immediately noticed that I was greeted only by cold stares from the female clerks, and the male employees could barely contain their laughter as they said good morning. Miss Wilkins, a dignified American who was secretary to the consul, intercepted me in the hall. Drawing herself up to her full height, she looked at me as if I were some revolting insect.

"There are some *persons* waiting to see you in your

office," she said, accenting the word with revulsion. "And when you've finished, the consul wants to talk with you."

All I can say is that I was completely unprepared for the scene awaiting me. There, seated around my desk, were four of the most well-known madames from Belem's Red Light District. Moreover, they had asked for me by name and had refused to speak to anyone else. They were dressed in ankle-length, red-and-blue silk dresses and wore heavy rouge. There could be no mistaking their profession.

Realizing that because of my apparent association with known ladies of the evening my days in the Foreign Service were probably drawing to a close, I decided to make the best of the situation. I bowed from the waist, "Distinguished ladies! To what do I owe the honor of your visit?"

"*O Senhor* Consul," they all began at once. My office door was slightly ajar, and I detected an unusually large gathering of my male colleagues at the water cooler in the hall. "It is about the disgraceful actions of your employee," Madame Ondina said. "And the great damage he has caused to our houses," Madame Ze Ze added. "It happened last Saturday night. Surely the police have already been in touch with you about it."

I was dumbfounded. "No, dear ladies, I have not heard from the police. Could you perhaps be a bit more specific?"

"Well," Madame Celestina continued, "around midnight your employee, *O Senhor* McDougal, who is also an American citizen, came into my house in a very drunken condition. Later, when asked to pay, he smashed the large mirror in my salon with a beer bottle."

According to Madame Ze Ze, it was after the police were called that the real damages occurred. It seems that when a truck filled with policemen arrived to arrest McDougal, he managed to climb through a small opening in a back room and got onto the roof, followed by five or six policemen. The houses in the district were built of sun-dried brick and stucco. They were set wall to wall and had slanting roofs composed of red clay tile, each connected to a neighboring one of the same fragile material. During the chase across the roof tops, parts of the roofs of four houses slid off onto the street.

McDougal was apprehended and taken away by the police. But the early light of dawn revealed a mass of broken tiles in the street along practically the entire length of one of the Red Light district's main thoroughfares.

"It was not only my roof, *O Senhor* Consul," lamented Madame Ondina through her tears, "but a piece of the roof fell upon my new record player and broke my best record. It was *La Paloma* by Miss Lily Pons—Miss Pons is American, no? It is very necessary for my business that I have another record by Miss Pons!"

McDougal had obviously spread the word throughout the district that not only was he an American citizen but that he also was an employee of the American consulate and working directly under my supervision. I was deemed the man holding the purse for damage payments, since I was depicted as his boss, and everybody knew that the Americans were rich.

The madames were incredulous when I told them the facts about McDougal's claims, but they finally left the consulate only to be replaced in the afternoon by one, *O Senhor* Osvaldo Fonseca and his lawyer. Fonseca averred, in a document drawn up by his attorney, that while in the act of relieving himself against the outside wall of the Waldorf Club in the district, that he had, suddenly and without prior warning, been struck on the head, neck, and other parts of the body from above by several pieces of falling tiles—thereby rendering him sick, sore, lame, and disordered. *O Senhor* Fonseca asked for one thousand dollars.

He also left the consulate in a livid rage when confronted with the information that McDougal was neither American nor employee, and that we would not pay.

I never saw McDougal again, but his legacy remained to haunt me throughout my remaining days in Belem. It was a rare day when I was not greeted on the streets profusely, and by name, by one or more of Brazil's most notorious madames. Unfortunately, this sometimes happened when I was accompanied by some visiting dignitary. I fear my friends spake evil of me in the market place.

Then came the wonderful day when I received notice of my transfer. After over two and a half years in Belem, I was being sent to Budapest to help reopen the consulate there after World War II. As I was clearing out my office, prior to packing my bags, a messenger placed a soiled envelope on my desk. I immediately handed it to the secretary.

"Miss Mello, my replacement will be arriving from Washington in a few days. Will you please see that he gets this?"

On the back of the envelope was written, "From Simon Bolivar McDougal—in Jail."

A QUESTION OF MURDER

A QUESTION OF MURDER

I couldn't say precisely when I made up my mind to kill Rajnal. It could have been on the day when I learned that Magda had been murdered. It may have been when Wilhelmina told me that the political police wanted her to bring them a floor plan of my apartment, and to let them know the next time I would be away overnight, by telephoning a certain number. Rajnal is dead, and so is Wilhelmina now, so my reference to her part in the affair can bring her no harm.

Wilhelmina, a fat and jolly, elderly peasant woman, was my cook and housekeeper in Budapest, Hungary in 1946. Magda, in her early twenties, brunette and beautiful, had been my girlfriend for almost a year when she was killed by the political police.

When I arrived in the country to take up my duties as an economic officer in the American Legation, it was practically impossible to find an apartment. The bombs during

World War II had taken a heavy toll in central Europe. A few houses were available, but they were reserved by the legation for the married officers, so I had the very difficult task of finding an alternative to a cramped hotel room. It was almost two months before I learned through a friend at the British Consulate that a local textile engineer had been granted an immigration visa for England. He was leaving behind a completely furnished apartment in a better part of the city.

It was only when I hurried to see the engineer that I found out just how completely furnished the apartment really was. He adamantly refused to rent to me unless I would agree to keep Wilhelmina, his housekeeper for many years, and Magda, his girlfriend. He had decided not to marry Magda, but she had no family and he didn't want to put her out on the street. I rented the apartment. It was on the ground floor of a three-story building and had five rooms, a terrace, a large garden, and three entrances, including one through the basement.

I suppose that, technically, one could say that I acquired both Wilhelmina and Magda as part of a real estate transaction, but this would be misleading. It would suggest that I heartlessly considered them to be mere chattel, which was not the case. In fact, I fell deeply in love with Magda, and she fully reciprocated my feelings. We eventually made plans to make our relationship permanent.

Shortly after I moved into the apartment, Magda returned one evening from the small photography shop where she worked and told me that she had been called to the office of the political police which, as in all Communist lands, is required to stamp out any anti-Communist sentiments among the local population and to monitor the activities of all foreigners in the country. She was brought to a dingy room in the police building. She was questioned at length by a young man in civilian dress, speaking the local language and some English with a strong Russian accent. He said that his name was Rajnal, and that Magda would be required to meet with him every two weeks to give him information about my activities. He wanted to know where I went, what social engagements I had, and, especially, the names and addresses of any local people with whom I had contact. He would be very interested in any letters which I received or wrote and would, later, provide her with a small camera to photograph any letters and other documents I might bring home from my office. He also warned her not to let me find out about her assignment.

Magda said that Rajnal had reddish brown hair and chain smoked Russian cigarettes. She noticed that he carried a small pistol in a shoulder holster during the interview. She faithfully told me all that transpired at the meeting, and we both fully realized the danger she faced should her interrogator learn that she had confided in me.

Since my work at the legation consisted of routine economic and commercial reporting—nothing secret or even confidential—I told Magda to cooperate with Rajnal. She should give him any information that he wanted. I had nothing to hide.

For about six months, all went well. Magda would make her regular reports to Rajnal and then inform me of the details of the meetings. Then one day she failed to return from the police building. The next morning, I telephoned her employer at the photography shop, and Wilhelmina went to see several of Magda's girlfriends. All our inquiries were in vain; Magda had disappeared. I, of course, notified the regular police that she "had failed to return to the apartment from her place of work," knowing full well that they would do nothing.

I learned of Magda's death a few weeks later from a

receptionist at the French Consulate. The receptionist was a local woman who had been arrested by the political police and spent several days in the prison where Magda was held. She told me that one morning she had seen the police remove Magda's bruised body through a rear door.

Both Wilhelmina and I were stricken with grief. Wilhelmina looked upon Magda as a daughter, and it took her some time to realize that Magda was never coming back. I could surmise that Magda, who was never one to pay too much attention to detail, had failed to report some trivial item in our daily program and that Rajnal had found out about it. I could not, however, understand how he could have found out. Magda and I had always discussed such things outside the apartment which, I always assumed, contained hidden microphones, and we never told Wilhelmina of her relations with the political police. Perhaps Rajnal had suspected that Magda was reporting to me about their meetings. Such suspicions in Communist countries are quite sufficient to bring about arrests and summary executions.

I was not surprised when Wilhelmina told me several weeks later that she had been called to the office of the political police. She had met with Rajnal and received instructions similar to those which he had given to Magda. I decided then and there that, as soon as possible, I would dismiss Wilhelmina and look for other quarters. The risks for her were too great. In the meantime, I asked her to be extremely careful to give Rajnal all of the information that he required—to withhold nothing and never to say or do anything which would let him know that I was aware of their meetings. She agreed but, simple soul that she was, I could never be certain that she understood the danger.

One summer morning Wilhelmina was serving me breakfast in the garden when she suddenly burst into tears.

"What is it, Wilhelmina? Are you ill?" We spoke German, which was her native tongue and which we both spoke better than the local language.

"No, Herr Konsul, but something terrible happened yesterday when I met with that horrible man, Rajnal!"

She told me that she was required to draw a floor plan of the apartment, showing exactly where each piece of furniture was located and to deliver the drawing to him the following week. He had mentioned a clothes closet in my bedroom, and I recalled that Magda had once reported to him that I sometimes kept my briefcase there. She didn't know that the only things in the briefcase were my pipe, tobacco, and a newspaper.

"Don't be upset. Simply sit down and draw the plan. I'll get the pencil and paper for you after coffee."

"But, Herr Konsul." She was crying. "I can't draw. I could never even draw a straight line!"

Then she told me that Rajnal wanted her to telephone him anytime she knew that I would be away from the apartment overnight.

I spent most of that Sunday drawing the layout of the apartment and, as I worked, a plan began to take shape in my mind—a plan to kill Rajnal. Obviously, someone wanted to enter the apartment while I was away, and my guess was that it would be Rajnal himself. The locks could be easily picked, or perhaps he had a key. I finished the drawing and instructed Wilhelmina to put iodine on her right hand and to bandage it thoroughly shortly before her next meeting with Rajnal. I did not want her to do further art work in his office. She would tell him that she had burned her hand in the kitchen and couldn't hold a pencil.

Wilhelmina's rendezvous with Rajnal went as expected. He even complimented her on the drawing. I took the first step of my plan by borrowing a Colt .45 Army service pistol and a full clip of ammunition from a sergeant in the legation guard. I explained that I wanted to do some target practice in the country. My next step was to tell Wilhelmina on Wednesday that I would be taking a trip with a friend on the coming Friday to a town in the southern part of the country. I told her that I would leave in the late afternoon, spending Friday night in the town and returning on Saturday. She was delighted because she could spend Friday night with friends in a nearby village and bring back some fresh eggs the next morning. I reminded her to inform Rajnal of my absence.

Late Friday afternoon, I drove in a legation car to the apartment and made a big show of picking up a suitcase and a thermos of coffee. Wilhelmina was still at the apartment and would leave a few hours later. I drove in a round-about way back to the legation garage. The sergeant on duty was surprised when I told him that I was through with the car and that I would pick up my suitcase the next day. I took the coffee with me.

Daylight was gone when I let myself into the apartment by the basement door, having walked back through side streets to make sure that I was not followed. A street lamp shining through a window enabled me to move around without a light. I checked the papers on my desk, as well as my briefcase in the clothes closet. Nothing had been disturbed. I took the pistol and the thermos into the bedroom and settled comfortably in an easy chair. The bedroom door was open, giving me a clear view of the living room. I was certain that the intruder would come straight to the closet and my briefcase. My chair was placed so he could not see me—until it was too late.

As I jacked a bullet into the chamber of the .45 and clicked the safety off, my thoughts wandered. I recalled my law school days, where I had made by best grades in criminal law. In America, if all of the facts were known to a judge and jury, what I was about to do would be first degree murder. All the elements were there—motive, premeditation, the planning and the act. But this was not America, and all of the facts would never be known. I would be dealing with a common, armed housebreaker. It would be self-defense. Oh, I was sure that Rajnal would bring along his little pistol in the shoulder holster. It was probably a 7.65 mm Walther or Beretta, the equivalent of an American .32 caliber, deadly at close range but not very accurate. Guns worn in shoulder holsters usually have short barrels. I hoped my diplomatic passport, though no defense to a murder charge, would be of help when I pleaded self-defense against an armed intruder.

It was ten p.m. I placed the pistol within easy reach and walked around the bedroom to stretch my legs. I didn't expect Rajnal before midnight, but I was prepared. My thoughts went back to my childhood in Texas. I remembered Tom Polk, an old-time Texas lawman who was a close friend of my family. He had taught me to shoot when I was fifteen years old. Mr. Tom didn't waste time and ammunition by shooting tin cans. He had me begin with his .38 Special and a life-sized cardboard dummy at thirty yards. I remembered Mr. Tom's advice to shoot for the heart. That is what I planned to do. If possible, I would first tell Rajnal that I was going to kill him to avenge Magda's death. Magda would have liked that.

Eleven p.m. I took out the slip of paper on which I had written the telephone number of the American legation. As soon as I was certain that Rajnal was dead, I would telephone the legation and have the duty officer and another American colleague from the consulate come to the apartment before I called the regular police to report the death of an armed burglar. The neighborhood was quiet; I wished I could turn on the radio. My left foot developed a cramp. I sipped some coffee from the thermos lid and tried to relax.

Midnight. Somewhere in the old part of the city, a clock struck six times. I looked at my watch. Typical Communist efficiency—not even the public clocks work. I was considering slipping into the kitchen to look for a piece of bread when I heard several soft taps on the terrace—like cushioned footsteps. I gripped the pistol and waited. Then I heard the "meow" and realized that it was the neighbor's cat. The nerves at the back of my neck were taut. I massaged them for a while. I took off my shoes and wriggled my toes to improve the circulation.

One a.m. It was so quiet in the apartment and on the street that, despite the coffee, it was becoming difficult to keep awake. I was almost dozing when the telephone rang! It was on the table beside me but, of course, I didn't pick up the receiver. So, I thought, it's Rajnal calling to make sure that no one is in. It rang for a few seconds and then stopped. Now I could expect a visitor soon. I walked around the bedroom again and checked the safety before resuming my vigil. My thoughts began again. I would probably resign from the Foreign Service, return to Texas and go into private business-or maybe open a law office. I was still young, but I was beginning to doubt that I could spend the rest of my working life outside my own country. Anyway, after this was over, I would probably be kicked out of the Service.

Two a.m. I drank the last of the coffee and thought about food, but I dared not go to the kitchen. My thoughts turned to Wilhelmina. Just yesterday she had told me that one day soon the Americans would start bombing Communist Europe. I suppose she believed this because all the local papers and newscasts were filled with anti-American venom, charging the United States with planning war. She had lived through the bombings of World War II and probably thought it only natural that the holocaust should start again.

"But, Herr Konsul," she had said, "you will know before the bombing planes come, and I would be very thankful to you if you would notify the bombers to watch out, when they get over this place, for a large 'W' made from white bedsheets spread on the ground. Tell them please not to drop any bombs where Wilhelmina will be!" I solemnly promised to relay her wishes to the Air Force. I again had to massage the back of my neck. All was quiet.

Three a.m. I could hardly keep my eyes open. I went into the bathroom and was about to wash my face, when I realized that the running water would make too much noise. Regardless of what happened, I would dismiss Wilhelmina as soon as possible and move back into a hotel room until a transfer came through or until I resigned—or until I was fired. I could no longer take the chance that she would meet the same fate as Magda. I went back to the chair and waited, pistol in hand.

Four a.m. For the first time I began to wonder if Rajnal would come. Then I began to think that perhaps he had learned somehow that Wilhelmina had kept me informed. I cursed myself for not having dismissed her earlier. I should have let her go immediately after Magda's death, but it was too late to worry about that now. I peered through the bedroom window. Nothing was moving on the street. The clock in the old town again struck six.

Five a.m. It would soon be daylight. A horse-drawn cart with wooden wheels clattered down the street. There was the clang of a milk can. Somewhere in the building, an alarm clock rang. I put on my shoes but decided to wait another hour.

Six a.m. This time the clock in the old town was correct, but a few minutes late. There was already some movement on the street. A door slammed in the apartment upstairs. I put the pistol aside and went into the kitchen to make my breakfast.

Rajnal had not come.

The following week, I dismissed Wilhelmina, who returned to her village to work for a German farm family. I never saw her again. I moved into a hotel and lived there for the remainder of my assignment. The hotel personnel were professionals at reporting to the political police: they never told me about it, and I was delighted.

I didn't kill Rajnal, but his Russian cigarettes did the job for me. A few years later, while serving at another post in South America, I learned that Rajnal had died in a hospital while undergoing an operation for lung cancer.

Had Rajnal showed up in my apartment, would I have pulled the trigger? It's a question I would really prefer not to answer. I would probably lie.

SOLOMON'S RETURN

SOLOMON'S RETURN

Sol looked me up at the consulate in Frankfurt as soon as he arrived. I had known him in New York, where he owned a men's clothing store. This was his first journey to Europe since the end of the war. Although several years had passed since World War II, he was extremely nervous about coming back to Germany because of his Jewish background. He insisted on registering at the consulate and listing his hotel addresses and telephone numbers, even though he planned to be in Germany for only four days. He repeatedly inquired if we thought it would be dangerous for him to travel in southern Germany, and, despite our reassurances, was still apprehensive. Thus I agreed to accompany him for a day's visit to his native village, in the Black Forest.

Sol's father had been a coal merchant in the village for many years and had owned a nice house on the main street. He foresaw the Nazi rise to power and, several years before the war, sent Solomon, an only child, to live with relatives in New York. He had planned to sell his business and later, together with Sol's mother, Augusta, join Sol in New York. It was not to be. Both were murdered in Auschwitz. Sol completed his education in the United States, became a citizen, married, and started a family.

It was nearing noon when we entered the village in our rented car. Sol immediately began pointing out familiar scenes and landmarks of his childhood. "That house there on the corner is where my cousin lived. He and his family of four were murdered by the Nazis. The bridge there over the little stream is where my friends and I used to fish after school. Of course we caught only minnows, but it was fun. There where the vacant lot is my father had his coal warehouse. He used to deliver the coal in a small pushcart. Many of his customers in the poor section of town usually couldn't pay, but my father always saw to it that they had enough fuel for the winter. He said it was his way of contributing something to his village."

We stopped in front of the local *gasthaus*, which had rooms to let and a restaurant. "The old owner of this place was a friend of my father. He's probably dead now. I was in school with his son. I see by the sign that the son is now the proprietor. He was one of the first in the village to join the Nazi party."

The restaurant was not crowded, and Sol and I sat at a table near the bar. "Is Manfred here?" Sol asked the young waiter.

"Why, yes, I believe he is," the waiter said, giving us a puzzled look.

"Tell him that Solomon is here and would like to see him," Sol said. "Meantime, bring us two beers and the menu."

The youth disappeared behind a curtain near the bar. After a few minutes, the curtain parted slightly for a second, but no one appeared. A short time later the waiter came with our beer. "I'm sorry," he said with a smile, "I made a mistake. Herr Manfred is out of town at the moment, and I don't know when he will return."

"It's all right," Sol replied. "I'll see him another time."

As we were finishing lunch, we saw our young waiter don hat and jacket and leave through a side door. "He's here, of course," Sol said, "but he doesn't want to see me. The whole town will now learn that I am here."

"Why did you come back, Sol?" I asked. He had told me that he no longer had relatives living in the area.

"Well, of course I wanted to see the old town and the places where I spent my childhood, but I really came to see Oma Seiler," Sol replied. "Oma Seiler is old now and almost blind. She was a good friend of my family. When the Gestapo started gathering the few Jews of the village for deportation, she and her husband and her daughter managed to hide my mother and father for several weeks in their attic. Oma saw to it that mother and father had food, but one day they ran out of salt and, since it was market day and the town was filled with farmers selling their vegetables, my father thought it would be safe to go a few blocks from the house to buy salt and a few apples. Someone recognized him on the street and informed the Gestapo. Oma Seiler's daughter saw them leading him away and ran back to the house to warn mother. They knew that the Gestapo would soon come to the house. Instead of trying to escape, my mother simply packed a few of her meager belongings into a small bag and waited. After the war, I was informed by the Red Cross that they both were murdered at Auschwitz.

"The Seilers paid a terrible price for their bravery. Oma, her husband, and her daughter were arrested and tortured. Her husband was released after a few months and sent to the Russian front, where he was killed. She and the girl spent over a year in prison. Oma Seiler wrote me that she has a package for me—a package given to her by my mother. I guess you could say that I came back for the package."

After lunch, we decided to walk to Oma Seiler's house, which was at the end of the main street, and on the way we stopped to see the house where Sol was born. It was a large two-story house, but the nameplate under the doorbell showed that it was occupied by only one family. Sol peered at the name. "Meier. Meier. Ah yes! I remember the family well. The old man was the village *gauleiter*—one of the first Nazis. This would be his son." Sol pressed the bell a few times, and a young, blonde woman opened the door.

"Frau Meier?" Sol asked.

The blonde woman smiled. "Yes. Ursula Meier."

"Frau Meier, I'm Solomon. I used to live here."

The smile on the woman's face was quickly replaced by a look of fear. "Why, er, yes," she finally stammered. "I know you, Solomon. Don't you remember? I was Ursula Hatz. We were in school together. Look, Solomon, if you've come about the house, er, that is, you know my husband and I bought the house and . .."

"No. No. I didn't come to try to get the house back," Sol said. "I've been fully paid for the house. The German government paid me. I just wanted to show my friend where I was born."

Frau Meier, still very nervous, showed us through the house and was visibly relieved when we left.

The street was almost deserted as we walked toward Oma Seiler's house. We saw a man approaching, dressed in a dirty, ragged army coat and a soiled kepi of the type worn by German soldiers. One sleeve of the coat was folded and pinned, indicating that he had lost an arm. He walked unsteadily, and the top of a wine bottle protruding from a coat pocket marked him as the village drunk. He stopped a few yards in front of us, blocking our passage, and stared intently at Sol. Suddenly the bewhiskered face broke into a broad grin. "Solomon!" he shouted. "Solomon! It's you, isn't it? You've come back! Remember me? I'm Karl."

"Yes, I remember you, Karl. How are you?" Turning to me, Sol added in English, "He was the most brilliant boy in my class. He was not a Nazi."

"Oh, not too good, Solomon." Karl pointed to his empty sleeve. "I got this in France from the Americans and was in the hospital for a few years with a head wound. I get by now with a little pension from the government. I never got married or anything. Did you come back to stay, Solomon?"

"No," Sol replied, "I'm just here for a visit."

Karl looked down at his ill-fitting shoes for a moment, and when he raised his head there were tears in his eyes. "I'm sorry, Solomon," he said. "I mean—I'm sorry for what happened to your parents and all. I wish you would come back and live in the village again, Solomon. We need you here to remind us of what happened. You are our conscience."

We shook hands with Karl and continued down the street. We had gone only a short distance when we heard him shout at the top of his voice, "You are our conscience Solomon! You are our conscience!"

When we rang Oma Seiler's bell, the door was opened by a young girl. "Does Oma Seiler still live here?" Sol asked.

"Yes," the girl said, "I'm her granddaughter. Do you wish to see her? Come, she's in her room upstairs."

We followed the girl to a small room where a very old woman with thick eyeglasses sat in an overstuffed chair. She tapped the floor with her cane. "Who is it, child? Bring them closer so I can see," she whispered.

"It's Solomon, Oma," Sol said in a loud voice, since the old woman was obviously partially deaf. "I've come back. I brought a friend."

"Sol! You finally came. You received my letter. Sit and let us talk. I'm glad you came because, as you can see, I haven't much time left." As she turned her head for Sol to kiss her cheek, she touched a hideous scar on the side of her face. "This is from the Gestapo," she said matter of factly.

They talked for a long while. Life in the village before the war; the coming of the Nazis, who was killed; who survived; the French occupation; the hunger; the fear. Oma related the story of Sol's parents. "I remember Augusta's exact words when we tried to persuade her to flee before the Gestapo came. She said, 'No, Johann and I have been together too long. I'll wait. Maybe we can be together again.' She packed a bag and waited. She was sitting right by the door with her bag between her knees when they came."

We could see that the old woman was tiring, and, as we prepared to leave, she tapped the floor loudly with the cane. "Girl!" she shouted, "bring the package!"

The girl left the room and returned with a small parcel which she handed to Sol. I noticed that his hands trembled as he opened it. Inside was a small circular wooden frame holding a lovely piece of embroidered linen. The blue thread was arranged, against a white background, to depict a dove in flight, but it was unfinished. The thread was still in the needle. "That's as far as she got before they came for her," Oma said. "When she heard the knock on the door, she handed it to me and said I should give it to you. She said you would be back."

Over Oma's protest, Sol left a considerable sum of money in her lap, and we said goodbye.

As we were driving back to Frankfurt, I asked Sol what he would do with the unfinished needlework.

"I'll bring it to my daughter, Carol. She will finish it."

AN EPITAPH
FOR ALI

AN EPITAPH FOR ALI

We buried Ali on a gentle hillside in the Old Cemetery in Budapest, Hungary on a misty autumn day in 1947. So far as I know, his grave is marked only by a simple stone slab bearing his real name and the dates:

Lunsud J. Goode
Born 1893—Died Oct. 13, 1947

It's not an appropriate epitaph for a hero. Of course, Ali would scoff at such a claim, for he was very modest. But I think that another line should be added to the stone. I would have it read, "An American Citizen Who Died for His Country."

Ali's funeral was supposed to be a simple one, as he had no religious affiliation. But as the coffin was being carried by a few friends to his final resting place in Buda, a group of Hungarian gypsies suddenly appeared. They carried their musical instruments and followed the coffin all the way to the open grave—playing slow, mournful, beautiful gypsy music. They had come, uninvited but most welcome, to give Ali a rare honor in his last rest. Ali was well known in Budapest's night life, and the gypsies considered him as one of their own.

Ali was a black man. He grew up in the slums of Boston, where his parents died when he was about ten years old. He never knew exactly where or when he was born. He learned to fight in the streets and alleys and in his early youth became a professional boxer. He never made the Big Time because he was too short and had no expert training, but he made a living of sorts in the early years of his manhood by fighting preliminary bouts along the East Coast.

Sometime in the 1920s, Ali went to Europe with a couple of fighters to stage exhibition bouts. The venture failed, however, and he was stranded in Paris without enough money for food. He decided to give up boxing for some other branch of show business.

He met a Hungarian promoter in Paris who was putting together a travelling vaudeville show. Ali couldn't sing or act, but as a boy he had danced in the streets of Boston for coins, so he was signed on and billed as a famous American tap dancer. As he once told me, his act was never a real threat to Fred Astaire, but he could do a fairly good buck-and-wing.

Dame Fortune, however, continued to withhold her smile from Ali. The group opened in Budapest. The show was a failure; the theater cancelled the contract, and the promoter disappeared without paying. This was in 1930. America was still deep in the big Depression, and Ali decided to stay on in Budapest and look for a job not connected with show business.

A black person was a rarity in Budapest, and racial discrimination against blacks did not exist in Hungary. On the contrary, Ali's color landed him a job on his very first try. His new employer, the owner of a cafe, believed for several years that Ali was a Moor from Morocco.

Hungarians have an abiding, unshakable belief, learned in the cradle and certified by the great coffee houses in Budapest: A good cup of coffee, of perfect flavor, delicate body and superb aroma, must be brewed by a dark-skinned native of Turkey, Morocco or other exotic land. Any cafe having such a man was assured of an elite clientele. So it was that Ali became the coffee brewer and coffee server in the most popular cafe and bar on Vaci Street in Budapest.

Of course, the management could never permit him to be called Lunsud Goode, so he was given an embroidered vest, a red fez, complete with tassel, and a new name, Ali—a name shared with the adopted son of Mohammed and all of the professional coffee servers in Hungary. But there was only one American Ali in Budapest.

Ali was quick to learn, and he soon became a bartender, in addition to his coffee duties. He also learned Hungarian and eventually married a Hungarian girl. He was well known in Budapest and, as the years passed, worked in many different bars, night clubs and cafes. Shortly before World War II, he became the chief bartender and coffee man in the Bristol, one of Budapest's finest hotels.

The American consulate in Budapest was reopened in the summer of 1945 amid the debris left by the second World War. After the war, Hungary was occupied and controlled completely by the Russian military, and the communist party was already beginning plans in 1945 to take over the government. Almost every day crowds marched past the consulate carrying red flags and banners reading, "Down with America! Death to Truman! Long Live Stalin!" Russian soldiers were murdering, raping and looting nightly in Budapest.

I was a young consular officer assigned to issue passports and repatriate those American citizens who had been trapped by the war in Hungary and who wished to return to the United States. Ali was one of my first customers. He and his wife—they had no children—had spent the war years in an internment camp in Budapest. He was about 52 years old when I met him and his wife a few years younger. He still had his old American passport, and the consular files verified his story and his claim to American citizenship. I gave him a new passport and explained that we could issue a visa to his wife when they were ready to leave for the USA.

I strongly urged Ali to hasten his departure for the United States before a communist government was formed which would have the power to prevent his wife, as a Hungarian citizen, from leaving the country. But he said that his life savings had been stolen when Russian soldiers had looted his apartment. He had reopened the bar and cafe at the Bristol and wanted to get some money together for living expenses while looking for a job in the United States. He had no known relatives and had decided to go to New Orleans.

The summer passed, and each month of 1946 saw a gradual strengthening of the communist rule in Hungary. I received frequent visits from Ali at the consulate and saw him occasionally at his bar. Each time he would flash a wide grin and say, "Just a few more weeks now, Mr. Consul! Just a few more weeks and we'll be ready to go."

By mid-1947, the communist campaign of terror had reached a new peak. The secret police and the Russians in Hungary were arresting and murdering suspected "enemies of the people" in Budapest prisons. No family was immune to the midnight knock on the door, which could mean death or deportation to the Soviet Union for slave labor. The huge concentration camps around Budapest were being filled with people, many of whom had been liberated just two years before from the Nazi prisons in Germany and Poland.

All of the professions, trades, and labor groups in Hungary fell under the rigid control of the communist party—a control which eventually included Ali's profession. A trade syndicate of bar and coffee house employees was formed, and Ali had to join or lose his job.

He continued to delay his departure for the United States.

I knew that Ali was in serious trouble the moment he stepped into my office that day. It was a cool October morning, but there were drops of sweat on his forehead. He was wearing his little white American sailor hat, which he always wore when not on duty at his bar, and he tried hard to look unworried, but his voice gave him away.

"Mr. Consul, I had a visit last night from some people. They want to make trouble for me. They want me to march in a communist parade through the streets of Budapest tomorrow afternoon. Can you get me and my wife out of here? We'd like to go as soon as possible."

The communist union had sent a delegation to order Ali to be on hand the next day at 4 o'clock in the afternoon. He was expected to march at the forefront of a mammoth communist parade. Moreover, he would be carrying a large red-lettered sign. The sign would read, "Down with America! Death to Truman! Long Live Stalin!"

As a well-known American in Budapest, Ali's participation in such a denunciation of his country would be a great coup for communist propaganda.

"I told them that I'd let them know by noon tomorrow," he said. "Of course, they made it clear that if I say no, they will never let my wife leave Hungary—they will put her in a concentration camp."

I immediately checked with the consular officer in charge of issuing visas. There was no way we could get Ali's wife out of Hungary so quickly. She would need an exit permit from the communist government.

When I relayed this piece of bad news to Ali, tears came to his eyes. He brushed them away with the back of his hand and stood up. "Well, Mr. Consul, what should I do?" he asked.

Whether he was afraid of what my answer would be or whether he suddenly realized that it was a question which only he could answer, I shall never know. Before I could speak, he turned toward the door and said, "Well, maybe I can work something out."

That was the last time I saw Ali.

The next morning, about 11 o'clock, I received a note, delivered to me in the consulate by a messenger, from Ali's wife. It said that Ali had died during the night of a heart attack.

The communist parade that afternoon was about like most all of them are: The same old monotonous, stupid drivel. Nothing special.

A few months after the funeral, we sent Ali's widow to the United States to live with friends in the midwest. How she got out of communist Hungary in those difficult days is not important now. We simply carried out Ali's wishes. Before leaving Budapest, however, she came to see me in my office at the consulate to say goodbye. We spoke of Ali. I expressed my sympathy.

She blinked back her tears, reached into her handbag and handed me a small brown bottle bearing a label with a red skull and crossbones. "These are the pills like Lunsud took," she said, looking straight into my eyes. "I didn't show them to the doctor. Lunsud took several of them. It was a sudden heart attack."

"Of course," I said quickly. "Of course. It was a heart attack."

And it is so recorded, officially, in the records of the American consulate in Budapest.

THE
INHERITANCE

THE INHERITANCE

It was the end of the rainy season in North Brazil, but there was still an occasional unpredictable downpour. The tropical sun had begun its workday, and small wisps of steam spiraled from the wet cobblestone streets of the old port city. Little spurts of muddy water lurking beneath the loose stones soiled the cuffs of my white linen trousers as I made my way on foot toward the harbor and the study of Padre Affonso. I always enjoyed my visits with the old priest, whom I had met shortly after my arrival in the city as a young American vice consul. He was highly educated and spoke some English. He also kept a generous supply of cold Brahma Chopp beer in his kerosene-burning refrigerator.

The labyrinthine path which led me this time to Father Affonso had begun the previous year in a lawyer's office in New York City. The law firm was the executor of the last will and testament of the deceased Gastao Pereira, a Portuguese immigrant who had made a fortune in the United States. By his will, he left his entire estate, valued at approximately a million dollars, to his niece, Evangelina Frazao. If she was dead, then the entire estate would go to her illegitimate daughter, Elena.

The daughter was in a girl's home in Massachusetts operated by Catholic sisters, but a problem arose concerning the whereabouts of the little girl's mother, Evangelina Frazao. Boston police records showed that she had escaped from a women's correctional facility in Massachusetts several years before the death of her uncle, and no trace of her had been found.

One day, detectives working for the law firm discovered that several payments for the benefit of the child, Elena, had been received by the sisters at the home. The money had been sent by a Catholic charity organization in Sao Paulo, Brazil. Information gathered by the American consulate in Sao Paulo indicated that the charity had received the payments at irregular intervals over a period of several years from a priest, Padre Affonso Hidalgo in North Brazil. These findings eventually brought about a long, detailed letter from the American Embassy in Rio de Janeiro enclosing a copy of the will and instructing my consulate to investigate the matter with Padre Affonso with a view to locating the missing American heiress. A check with the Brazilian police and immigration officials had turned up no records of Evangelina Frazao.

Padre Affonso welcomed me effusively in his small, book-lined study. It was stifling hot, and the room smelled of mold. He turned on the small ceiling fan and brought out two bottles of beer. He assumed that I had come to discuss some rare books on Portuguese history, in which we both were interested. He seemed disappointed when I told him that this was an official visit.

"In what way, *O Senhor* Consul, can a very old, ignorant Brazilian priest be of service to the American government?" he asked, his ancient eyes twinkling with amusement.

I told him about the will and the instructions that we had received from the embassy. His expression did not change when I gave him the name, Evangelina Frazao, but he became visibly agitated when I mentioned Elena, the Catholic girls' home in Massachusetts and the money transfers.

"Tell me," he finally said after a long pause and a sip of beer, "do you have a photograph or a description of the woman—this Evangelina Frazao—and why was she in prison?"

I handed him a faded photograph. "We have only this copy of a very old mug-shot. The original was a very indistinct photo made many years ago when she entered the reform institution. It was not really a prison but a reform school for delinquent girls. She was serving a term for shoplifting and prostitution when she escaped. We really can't identify her from this picture, but we do have a description. She is now thirty years old, five feet five inches tall, light complexion, brown eyes, and the natural color of her hair is black. But, most important, there is a distinguishing physical feature: she has a crimson birthmark beginning on the lower right side of her neck and extending down to her right shoulder."

Padre Affonso sat silently for a while staring intently at the photo. Finally, looking straight into my eyes, he said, "*Senhor* Consul, I can tell you definitely that I do not know this woman. I have never seen her nor heard her name before. About the other thing—the money to the girls' home—you will understand that we of the church must respect certain confidences. Of course, this is a special situation." He paused for a few minutes in deep thought. "Give me a few days. Perhaps I can be of help. I'll send a message to you at the consulate if I have some news."

Exactly a week later, a small boy came to the consulate with a note from Padre Affonso inviting me to call on him. When I arrived at his study, I found him in a jovial mood in spite of the oppressive heat. We had two bottles of cold beer and discussed the events of the day. One never plunged precipitously into official matters with Padre Affonso. He opened a desk drawer and took out a slip of paper. "Do I understand correctly," he asked, "that the little girl, Elena, will inherit all of the property if her mother, Evangelina Frazao, is dead?"

"Yes," I replied. "That is correct. But there would have to be proof of her death, and that might be difficult since, as an escapee from a reform school, she would probably assume another name and obtain false identity papers. We have not yet checked the city death records here. Of course, under American law, if she is not found within a certain number of years, a court could declare her legally dead, but this procedure could take much time."

"I see. Well, I can refer you to someone here who can probably give you some information." He handed me the slip of paper. "She will be awaiting your visit—preferably this afternoon between four and six o'clock."

I should not really have been surprised at the name and address on the paper since, after all, we were seeking a person who was a known prostitute. Nevertheless, I gasped when I read it: Madam Carlotta, The Marajo Palace. The Palace, in the heart of the city's red-light district, was one of the largest and most luxurious bordellos in the world, and

Madam Carlotta was the most notorious bordello madam in South America.

I knocked on the mahogany door of the Marajo Palace at four p.m., and a servant took me immediately to Madam Carlotta's private office. I must confess that I was disappointed by Madam Carlotta's appearance. I had never met anyone who had seen her, but from the stories that I had heard, I was expecting to see a refined woman of great beauty and regal bearing. Instead, I was confronted by a middle-aged, blonde, rather fat, Brazilian woman of medium height, with very shrewd eyes. The premature lines on her hard face indicated many years as a "working girl" in her profession before ascending to the position of madam.

She remained seated before a large desk as she extended a hand bearing several diamond rings. "I am honored by your visit, O Senhor Consul," she said, offering a chair. "Padre Affonso has told me all about your request for information."

She spoke the Brazilian Portuguese with a slight accent. I noted that she occasionally used a Spanish word instead of Portuguese. "Thank you for receiving me, Senhora," I said. "From your nice accent, I gather that you are of Spanish origin."

She smiled and nodded. "Now, tell me about this woman whom you seek. I am told that you have her photo."

"Yes, we are trying to locate Evangelina Frazao, an American citizen, born in Boston, Massachusetts." I gave her the photograph. "We also have here a detailed description of her," I added, taking from my briefcase the embassy's letter.

She held up her hands. "That will not be necessary, Senhor Consul," she said in a soft voice, almost a whisper. "I knew this girl very well. She is dead." There was a far-away look in her eyes, and I thought that she would burst into tears, but she didn't. "Evangelina Frazao was one of my girls here for several years. She died on September fifth last year of pneumonia. She is buried in the Sao Tomas cemetery. I paid for the funeral myself."

I tried, unsuccessfully, to hide my astonishment. "Then she worked here under her real name?" I asked.

"She was known as Lina, but I knew her real name and her background. We were close friends, and she confided in me. The girl was not a criminal, *Senhor* Consul. I know that she was sent to a reform place for theft, but do you know what she stole, *Senhor* Consul? She stole a bottle of cough syrup from a drug store! She stole it because her child was sick, and she had no money to pay a doctor or to buy medicine. Oh, yes! I know about the little girl who was placed with the Catholic sisters when Lina was sent to that place. Lina's parents were dead. She knew that there was an uncle somewhere in the United States, but she didn't know where. She tried to support herself and the child by working as a prostitute on the streets of Boston. After escaping from the reform house, she came to Brazil because, being of Portuguese descent, she spoke the language and could mix with the Brazilians without attracting attention."

"But, *Senhora*," I interrupted, "do we have any proof that the dead girl was Evangelina Frazao—I mean a passport, an identity card or some other document?"

"You know, *Senhor* Consul, the girls who work here come from different parts of Brazil and even countries such as France, Spain and the United States. Most of them stay here only a short time, and only a few have official identity documents. Fortunately, I know all of the top officials here. Most of them are good customers. They take my word that my girls are who they say they are, and no questions are asked. But Lina did have a document." Madam Carlotta handed me a worn, yellow sheet of paper. It was a certificate, bearing the letterhead of the Massachusetts correctional institution. It certified that Evangelina Frazao had completed the sewing course at the reform school and was a qualified seamstress. There was no photograph attached. "Then there is this picture of her little girl, Elena." Madam Carlotta added, pointing to a photo, framed in silver, standing on her desk. "You may take it if you like."

"I don't believe we'll need the child's picture, *Senhora,*" I replied. "I will, however, take the seamstress' certificate, and I assume that there is a death certificate available?"

Madam Carlotta opened a drawer of her desk. "Here is a copy of the death certificate. You may take it, but I would like to have it returned to me when you have the official one. I intended to have it sent to the Catholic girls' home in Massachusetts." The document, signed by a local health official, stated that Evangelina Frazao, a U.S. citizen, seamstress by profession, had died of pneumonia. It was dated September fifth of the preceding year.

"*Senhora,*" I said, "perhaps you know why Evangelina did not send the money directly from here to the girls' home in Massachusetts instead of having it sent from Sao Paulo."

She stared for a moment at the child's picture on her desk. "*Senhor* Consul, Lina loved her little girl very much and had great hopes for the child's future. She lived in fear that the authorities would return her to the reform institution, but her greatest fear was that the girl would, one day, learn about her mother's past and her profession. The girls' home in Massachusetts was simply told that the child's mother had disappeared. They didn't know where Lina was, and she never communicated with them directly. She arranged with Padre Affonso to transfer the money from another city in order to conceal her whereabouts and her identity."

I put the papers into my briefcase and took my leave. The next day, a telegram was sent from the consulate to the American Embassy in Rio de Janeiro:

EVANGELINA FRAZAO DIED HERE
SEPTEMBER FIFTH LAST YEAR STOP
IDENTITY DOCUMENT AND CERTIFIED
COPY DEATH CERTIFICATE BEING SENT
BY DIPLOMATIC POUCH.

I again called on Madam Carlotta the following week. It was five o'clock in the afternoon, and the Palace was not yet open for the day's business. She welcomed me in her office as an old friend. She was dressed in a white linen skirt and a blue silk blouse fastened at the collar by a large diamond pin and appeared much more relaxed than on our first meeting. I returned the copy of the death certificate to her, apologized for the delay, and was about to leave, but she motioned me to a chair.

"*Senhor* Consul," she said, "it's been a long day. Please join me in a small glass of champagne." Without waiting for my reply, she pressed a button on her desk, and the huge, uniformed servant who had opened the door for me came into the room. "Joao," she said, "bring us an ice bucket, two glasses and a cold bottle of the Piper Heidsieck."

The champagne arrived. I thought it only proper to make small talk. I didn't want to inquire too closely into Madam Carlotta's background or her present life, so we talked about the weather. Yes, she agreed, the rains had ended early and, yes, she thought the heat was more oppressive than last year. "I really must get some more fans in this place," she said. "The sticky heat in here is almost unbearable." She unsnapped the diamond pin on her blue silk blouse and opened the collar wide. That's when I saw the crimson birthmark on the right side of her neck. I could see that it extended down to her right shoulder. I spilled most of the champagne from my glass, and my face apparently went so white that Madam Carlotta thought that I must be ill.

As soon as I recovered my voice, I assured her that it was only the heat, and that I was all right. I did my best to continue the conversation. "May I ask, *Senhora,* are you happy here in North Brazil? The climate is so different from that of Spain."

"Ah, *Senhor* Consul," Madam Carlotta smiled, "happiness and sorrow sometimes come in the same package. I am very happy for the little girl in America, but I am sorry that her mother is dead. Let us drink to the little girl's future."

I raised my glass.

A FRIEND IN CHICAGO

A FRIEND IN CHICAGO

I saw Sam's picture in the newspaper yesterday. It's been several years now since I've seen him in person, and he has put on some weight, but I recognized him at once.

My introduction to Sam came in the form of a garish business card handed to me by my secretary at the consulate in Naples, Italy. The card read, "Sam Natrelli, Good Used Cars." It gave the addresses of his two places of business, one in Gary, Indiana and one in Chicago, and contained the usual slogans associated with used-car enterprises. I was surprised to see that he didn't refer to himself as "Honest Sam."

"The *gentleman* says that he is an American citizen," the secretary said, accenting heavily the word "gentleman." "He wants to see you in connection with the passport which we issued to his sister a few weeks ago."

My job as passport officer at the consulate had to do with

the renewal of passports as well as investigating the American citizenship claims of first-time passport applicants from the Naples consular district. I didn't immediately remember the name, Natrelli, since my workload had been very heavy during the past month, so I consulted my files: "Natrelli, Giovanna. Age 27. Born in Naples. Derived American citizenship through parents. O.K. for passport." It had been a routine case with no complications. Giovanna was entitled to a passport, and one had been issued to her. The file showed that she had been living with an aunt in Naples since the death of her mother and that she would be going to Chicago to join her father and an older brother. Sam was the brother.

A consular officer, if he remains long in the service, sees many strange sights and meets many unusual people. I had been long enough in the service to attest to this fact. Even so, I was not really prepared for Sam.

"Hiya, Consul!" Sam shouted in a drillmaster voice. "I come here special to thank you for wot you done for m'sister. Without your help, she'd never of made it to the USA! She told me so herself. She'll be goin' back to Chi with me in a few days." Sam strode into my office amid a cloud of smoke from his expensive cigar and extended a hand with a blue-white diamond ring of at least three carats on the pinky. He was a short, swarthy man in his mid-thirties with black, bushy eyebrows and the onset of a paunch. The most remarkable thing was his manner of dress. He wore a gaudy pinstripe suit with a wide-lapel, two-button jacket and pleated trousers which were a few inches too long. He kept the jacket unbuttoned, exposing a white-on-white shirt starched to perfection and topped by a black bow tie. An equally starched white linen handkerchief peeked from the breast pocket next to a brilliant red carnation in the lapel buttonhole. The ensemble was completed by a dark felt

Borsalino hat with the brim turned down in front at a sinister angle.

As Sam seated himself in front of my desk, without removing the hat, I thought for a moment that I was confronted with a leading character direct from an old American gangster movie—or maybe even the real thing! But I quickly dismissed the thought, realizing that real mobsters no longer dressed or talked like that. At least the one I had recently seen on television testifying before a congressional crime committee didn't, and he had spoken better English than many college professors I know. So I accepted Sam as a jolly, expansive, entirely likeable, self-made, American businessman. He obviously had no formal education, but he was apparently successful in his business.

"Now, Consul," Sam said, without taking the cigar from his mouth, "you've done me a real big favor by fixin' up this passport thing for m'sister. Ya know, a coupla them shysters in Chi they told me it couldn't be done. Said she'd lost her Amurrican citizenry. But you done it! I ain't gonna ask no questions. All I wanna know now is what can I do for ya? Know what I mean? Ya want something here in Italy, or in the States, or anywheres else—you name it. You got it!"

I finally realized with horror that Sam truly believed that I had settled his sister's case by deviousness and that he was expected to make a "payoff" or, in plain English, a bribe. I stopped him before he could continue and did my best to explain that there were no favors involved and that I wanted nothing and would accept nothing. I could see from the expression on Sam's face that he was trying hard to understand, but he was so astonished that he took the cigar from his mouth and shook his head sadly. It was as if his innate faith in timeworn business traditions had been shattered.

It was my custom to spend some time, whenever

possible, outside the consulate with visiting American citizens. This not only permitted the taxpayers to see where, even if minuscule, a part of their taxes went. It also allowed me to keep in touch with current events at home, especially the football and baseball scores. So it was that I had Sam to dinner at my small apartment, overlooking the Bay of Naples, where Romola, my cook-housekeeper, prepared an excellent meal. Over brandy and cigars, Sam made it plain that he still believed that I, alone, was responsible for his sister's good fortune. Seeing that I would accept nothing in return, he set about advising me as to ways for advancing my career. He obviously was not pleased that one who could do the impossible for a member of his family should not occupy a greater station in life than a job as a vice consul.

"Now lissen, Consul! Th only way to get ahead in this biness you're in is to get some publicity. Know what I mean? Do somethin' that'll get yer name spread around, see? Ya gotta get yer pichure in the papers. That way you'll really make it big! Know what I mean?"

I enjoyed several visits from Sam in Naples, and the day before he and his sister left for Chicago, he came to my office and left another business card. "Lissen, Consul," he said, "one of these days you'll be comin' to Chi. Now when ya get there, I wantcha to call this special nummer here that I've wrote on the backa this card. Don't pay no mind to them other phone nummers—them's my car lots, and I may not be there. Remember now, I'll be lookin' for ya call, and if I ain't there, leave a phone nummer, an you'll hear from me."

I tucked the card into my wallet and said goodbye to Sam. The possibility that I would ever get to Chicago—or see Sam again—was remote indeed.

It can get very cold in Chicago in February. There are certain streets where, if you are walking north, the wind can blow a thousand needles into your face and sleet will freeze into your eyebrows. Chicago, like any big city where you are alone and know no one, can also be a very lonely place. How do I know these things? Exactly one year after saying goodbye to Sam in Naples, Italy, I was unpacking my suitcase in a small hotel in the middle of Chicago. I was there by courtesy, and at the expense, of the State Department in Washington, D.C., where I had been transferred after a normal tour of duty in Italy. The legal division to which I was assigned decided that it should have affidavits from certain immigrants from Europe. These people were scattered across the entire United States. Since it was winter and I was young, unencumbered by dependents, and not very bright, I was handed a list of names and addresses, some train and plane tickets and sent on my way.

Chicago was my third stop, after Boston and Cleveland. I had allocated two weeks for Chicago. After checking into a modestly priced hotel, I followed my usual practice and called on the local FBI office, where arrangements had been made for a desk and a secretary-notary. The secretary and I would sally forth each morning by taxi, locate our quarry, and get a signed statement on the spot. The work was slow, because most of the addresses which I had from the State Department were wrong, and this resulted in lengthy visits with innumerable relatives of the newcomers to America.

During my first week in Chicago I had no time to think of personal diversions. I met several of the FBI agents at the office. They were all nice fellows, but all were married and had homes in the suburbs to which they returned religiously each evening when not working on a special case. They didn't do much entertaining.

Saturday evening of my first week in Chicago arrived, and I was sitting in my room watching the snow falling outside my window. I decided to audit my finances before going to the grubby diner across the street for a beer and sandwich. I took out my wallet and emptied the contents on the bed, counted the few bills, and while returning them to the billfold, I found Sam's business card. I must confess to a slight feeling of shame as I read the card with the "special nummer" written on the back. The fact was that I had not thought of Sam since his visit in Naples. It was not late, so I picked up the telephone and asked the hotel operator to dial Sam's special number. He dialed, and a man's voice answered with just one word: "Yeah?"

"May I speak with Mr. Natrelli, please?"

"Sam ain't here. He's outta town. Whaddya want?"

I gave my name, but I could tell from the labored grunts on the other end of the line that the man was having spelling problems. I finally said, "Just tell Sam that the consul from Napoli is here and would like to see him." I gave the name of my hotel and the telephone number, hoping that the fellow could write numbers.

Exactly two minutes after I had put down the telephone, Sam called. "Hiya, Consul! So ya finally got here! Really great! Whatcha doin' in town? But no mind that now. We'll talk later. I know yer hotel, and I'm comin' right over. Ya didn't eat yet, didja? Great! I'll be in the lobby in 'bout thirty minutes. We're gonna go eat."

"But I understood your friend to say on the telephone that you were out of town."

"Ah, he don't know nothin'. Know what I mean?"

I was sitting in the lobby when Sam charged in. He was accompanied by a muscular young man dressed in a fashionable gray suit and carrying an overcoat on his arm.

"Well, how they treatin' you, Consul?" Sam asked, after giving me the embrace of a long-lost brother. He had on his usual pinstripe suit, bow tie and immaculate white-on-white shirt. The red carnation was also in place. "What kinda room ya got here?" He nodded when I affirmed that my room was comfortable but small.

On our way out of the hotel, Sam introduced the young man. "This is Harvey. He works with me in the biness." Harvey, who had remained standing by the lobby entrance, nodded and smiled but didn't say anything nor offer to shake hands. I noticed that he had a cauliflower ear. I assumed that Sam had a taxi waiting, but standing in front of the hotel was a new Fleetwood Cadillac with a driver, who was introduced as Vito. Vito didn't reply when I said hello.

We drove to a section of Chicago where there was one bar or nightclub next to the other seemingly for miles on end. I didn't know the city well, but I marvelled at the number of nightspots and at the great variety of entertainment which they advertised. We stopped before a bar which offered, among other things, "Lovely Ladies Dancing on the Bar While You Enjoy Your Drink!" I was beginning to feel the pangs of hunger and feared that Sam had chosen the wrong place for dinner. But I need not have worried. There were, indeed, topless ladies walking around on top of a large circular bar, while one of them played an excellent rendition of "Nola" on the accordion. The place was crowded, and several of the patrons and waiters greeted Sam loudly as we made our way to a back room. The small, quiet room had only one table, and it was set for four. A large bottle of Chianti Classico red wine was already in place, and Sam filled three glasses, while a buxom waitress took our orders. Harvey didn't drink.

We dined on excellent steaks. Harvey ate two. Neither Vito nor Harvey said a word during dinner. Sam, however, was his usual effervescent self. In reply to his questions about my presence in Chicago, I answered truthfully about my job, without telling that I worked out of the local FBI office. I didn't think that this was of any importance. In return, I inquired about the family and his used-car business. The family was well; Giovanna was going to night school to improve her English, and business was good.

"Lissen, Consul," Sam said during dinner, "You been to law school. Whyn't you get outta the govmint biness? Come out here and open a law office. I know some people here, and I can throw a lotta biness your way. We'll getcha some publicity—get ya pichure in the papers, and you'll make it big! Know what I mean?" I gave some evasive answer but promised to think it over, which seemed to satisfy him. The waitress brought the coffee, and Sam whispered something in her ear. Shortly we were joined by the girl with the accordion who, Sam said, was from Palermo. She entertained us with Italian folk songs until the wee hours.

Sam left me at my hotel after extracting a promise that I would join him and his family for dinner at his home. "I got some biness to take care of in New York next week, but I'll pick you up here at the hotel next Thursday at six o'clock. Giovanna wants to see you, and some of the boys'll be there. We'll have a real Italian meal! Know what I mean?"

The weather was better on Monday, and the secretary and I were able to get statements from almost all of my customers. I would be able to finish my work in Chicago in two or three more days. I was back at the office preparing to return to the hotel when Henry, one of the FBI agents, sauntered over to my desk. "Well, how's it going?" he asked by way of friendly conversation. Everyone in the office had been very busy during the past week with not much time for pleasantries.

"Not too bad. This little break in the weather helped a lot. I'll be able to wind up my work here ahead of schedule."

"Fine. By the way, what do you do for entertainment? Know anybody in Chicago?" Henry asked.

"Yes, I've got a friend here. Matter of fact we had a whale of a party Saturday night. Incidentally, he's big in the used-car business. If you ever need a good used car, I can recommend him." I took Sam's business card from my wallet and handed it to him.

Henry looked at the card, then he did a strange thing: He began opening and closing his mouth like a fish out of water, as if he were gasping for air. When he finally found his voice, he stared at me skeptically and said, "You know this guy? Where'd you meet him?"

I told Henry of Sam's visit to Naples and about his sister's passport. He uttered an obscenity and motioned me to a chair. I knew of course that something was wrong.

"Let me put it this way," Henry said. "Mr. Natrelli is not only big in used cars. He's also big in stolen cars; he's also big in drugs, illegal gambling, prostitution and very big in the protection racket. We've never been able to nab Sam, but we've got a file on him that's a foot thick, and we'll keep trying. He was formerly a member of a New York mob. Had some trouble with a rival gang there and came out here for his health."

I was correct in assuming that Henry also knew Vito and Harvey. "Sure, that would be Harvey Floyd and Vito Giovanetti. Harvey was once a promising heavyweight fighter in California until he was sent up for armed robbery. He's Sam's bodyguard, known to the mob of course as Pretty Boy. Vito is the worst of the lot. He's a born killer. He did time in New Jersey for manslaughter and has a couple of murders to his credit here, but, so far, we've not been able to pin him down. He's Sam's enforcer in the protection racket."

It had been a long day, but I had another surprise in store for me when I returned to the hotel. A very solicitous manager met me in the lobby. "Excuse me, sir," he said, wiping his eyeglasses nervously with a handkerchief, "we've prepared some rooms for you on the top floor. You'll be much more comfortable in the suite. The boy will take your things up when you are ready."

"Very kind of you," I replied, "but that will not be necessary. I'll not be staying as long as I had planned, and, frankly, the suite would be out of my price range."

"Oh, don't worry about that, sir. Your friend, Mr. Natrelli, is taking care of that. He's asked us to pass along all of your hotel bills to him. He also feels that you'd like the suite better than your present room. I'd consider it a personal favor, sir, if you'd take the suite."

It pained me to see the beads of perspiration form on the manager's forehead when I said no to the suite and demanded that he have my bill ready for me on Wednesday morning, making it clear that I would pay my own charges.

As I had predicted, the secretary and I were able to get the last of our affidavits finished on Tuesday afternoon. On Wednesday morning, I paid my hotel bill, said goodbye to Chicago and took a plane for Dallas. About Sam's invitation for an Italian dinner on Thursday evening? I took the coward's way out. I mailed a short note, with no return address, to Sam, saying that I had been unexpectedly called back to Washington to take on another job.

The years passed, with new posts, new assignments, new friends, and I forgot about Sam completely—that is until I saw his picture in the newspaper yesterday. As I said, I recognized him right away, even before I read his name in the caption, and even though he was lying in a pool of blood on a Chicago street, his beautiful white-on-white shirtfront stitched with little black bullet holes.

Sam finally made it big.

A LETTER
FOR CHARLEY

A LETTER FOR CHARLEY

It is the end of a beautiful late summer day. As twilight approaches, I sit alone with a small glass of wine in my study, surrounded by mementos of half a lifetime spent in various corners of the world. As I turn on the stereo, the soft melody of an old Victor Herbert tune begins to tug gently at my memory. A pleasant female voice is singing *Kiss Me Again*. The half-whispered words are like a lullaby, and my thoughts take the first steps of a familiar journey into the past. I remember Charley, for this was Charley's favorite song. And I remember Leila. Through the growing evening shadows I can see her again, dressed in her sequined gown, standing there on the little stage as she sang that song for Charley.

Charley arrived in Budapest a few weeks after I did. We were part of the staff sent there to reopen the American legation and the consulate after World War II. He was a young man at his first post, about the same age as I, slim, with curly blond hair and blue eyes shielded by a pair of metal-rimmed glasses.

Hungary was still in a state of chaos. The siege of Budapest had left a large part of the city in ruins. Thousands of people who had been in Nazi concentration camps were returning to the city and attempting to find shelter among the bombed-out buildings. They also had to cope with the Soviet occupation forces, who were still looting, raping, and murdering civilians.

Since adequate housing for American personnel was scarce, I invited Charley to move in with me. I had been fortunate enough to find a small apartment in the city, within walking distance of the consulate. The first thing he unpacked was a suitcase filled with books. He also brought a record player and a supply of records, including his Victor Herbert favorite.

A few bars, restaurants, and night clubs soon opened, with meager fare but with good music, and a group of young entertainers reopened the small variety theater just two blocks from our apartment. They had no stage furnishings but managed to assemble an excellent orchestra and several good singers. The costumes were made from curtains and drapes. I didn't know that the theater had opened until the day I had a visit from one of its company. I had just finished interviewing a passport applicant in my office when the secretary came in.

"There's someone from the variety theater here to see you, sir; she says it will only take a minute."

I grudgingly said yes and soon the door opened to admit a vision! Her raven hair, drawn together at the back of her neck, accentuated a pair of green eyes and a beautiful complexion. She was probably in her early twenties and had a perfect figure, covered by a dress much too thin for the prevailing weather.

"I am Leila," she said, with a dazzling smile before I could recover my voice. "I am singer at the variety theater."

Her request caused me almost as much consternation as did her beauty. Leila wanted an American parachute.

"You see," she said, "I have not a proper costume for singing my songs on the stage, but if you would perhaps have an American parachute here in your consulate which you would not need—now that the war is finished—I could make from it a very nice dress for myself."

I explained that I didn't have one at the moment. Then I recalled that Charley sometimes drank beer with one of the sergeants from the military attache's office. It was just possible the sergeant might be able to find one.

I don't know where or how Charley managed to get the parachute, but he did. The following evening we took it to the theater. I had described Leila in glowing terms, and Charley was looking forward to meeting her. The theater was giving performances only once a week, on Friday evenings. The other days were spent in rehearsals and in making repairs to the stage and the seats, badly damaged by a shell.

The entire troupe, including the orchestra members, were doing the carpentry themselves. When we arrived at the theater, we found Leila, with a red bandana around her hair, nailing some boards onto a stage prop. Several of her colleagues were similarly occupied. I introduced Charley, who presented Leila with the parachute. She was jubilant and gave both of us a big kiss.

Since none of us had eaten, we persuaded Leila to join us at the Apostles Bar and Restaurant for some beer and whatever the cook could prepare. Despite the poor quality of the food, it was a memorable meal. For Charley and Leila, it was the beginning of a love affair.

Leila was a Bulgarian. After finishing high school in Sofia, she had come to Budapest to live with a relative, and to take singing lessons. She wanted to become an opera star. She had been trapped in Budapest by the war, spending many days and nights in the cellars, surviving by eating horse meat and a few dried fruits. She later learned that most of the male members of her family in Bulgaria had been deported to concentration camps. She was anxiously awaiting word from her mother about their fate.

Within a month, work on the theater had made such progress that the troupe was performing twice a week, Tuesdays and Fridays. There was usually a large audience. The orchestra and singers learned many of the current popular American songs, and it was not unusual to hear hits such as *Don't Fence Me In, Deep in the heart of Texas*, and *As Time Goes By*.

Charley and Leila were soon spending almost all their spare time together. He would go to the theater and watch rehearsals, then take Leila to dinner. On Tuesdays and Fridays, it became established practice for Charley and me to attend the show in the evening, then go to the Apostles Bar, where we would wait for Leila to change and join us for a late supper. On Saturdays, Charley would get a jeep from the legation garage, and they would spend the weekend at Lillafured or some other village in the countryside. Charley's love for Leila gradually became almost an obsession. From all appearances, she fully returned his affection.

As predicted, the winter was hard. We managed to get a small coal-burning stove for the apartment, and Charley got one for the small room that Leila had rented. There was no heat in the theater, but each performance continued to be sold out—the audience sitting in heavy coats and sipping from bottles of plum brandy. Leila had made a magnificent gown from the parachute, decorating it with sequins which glittered in the spotlight. She also learned a few of Charley's favorite songs, including *Kiss Me Again.*

Winter passed, and spring was turning into lovely summer weather when Charley returned to the apartment that Sunday evening from his usual weekend with Leila. I saw immediately that this was to be a special occasion. He was exultant.

"Pull up a chair and sit!" He brought out a bottle. "I have wonderful news! Leila has finally said yes. We are going to be married."

His news was not exactly a surprise, but he had never talked with me about his plans. I felt that I should mention some of the consequences of his decision—especially how it would affect his career.

"Of course you know the rules, Charley. Since Leila is not an American citizen, you will be expected to submit your resignation to the State Department at the time you report your intention to marry a foreigner. They may not choose to accept your resignation—but what happens if they do?"

"Couldn't care less," Charley replied. "Leila means more to me than anything else in the whole world. I would take a job digging ditches if necessary. The only important thing is that we are to be married!"

"Fine, Charley. I know how you feel. And when will the big event take place?"

"We haven't set a date. I told her I would have to inform the department. She asked me not to report it yet. She's waiting for a letter from her mother in Bulgaria. I think she wants to have her mother come to Budapest for the ceremony."

It was about two weeks later, on a Friday morning, when Leila came to see me in my office at the consulate. When the secretary announced her, I assumed that she had come with the usual minor request for help in finding some stage prop or other. She was wearing a pair of dark sunglasses, but I could see that she had been weeping.

"I need your help," she said. "It's about Charley. I can't marry him."

"Why not?"

"I'm leaving tonight, after the show, for Bulgaria," she continued, ignoring my question.

"Have you told Charley?"

"No, and I can't. That is why I need your help. I have here a letter which I've written to Charley. Please read it." She handed me a small white envelope which contained a single sheet of paper. The letter was not a long one, and it was certainly no love letter.

> Dear Charley,
>
> I'm sorry I cannot marry you as I promised because I do not love you. I realize that what I did was wrong, but I promised to marry you only to get the visa to the United States of America. I wanted only to sing some day in the opera there and to get the American citizenship. Do not try to reach me. When you read this, I will be en route to Bulgaria. I am sorry.
>
> Leila

I read the letter and looked up to see Leila sitting uneasily in the chair, dabbing at her eyes. She was a picture of misery.

"Is this true—what you've written here to Charley?" I asked.

She shook her head. "No, it is not true. It is all a lie. I do love Charley very much, and I want to marry him. But I cannot."

She took other letters from her handbag. "I received these letters yesterday from Bulgaria. You see, after I finished school in Bulgaria, I became engaged to a boy from my village. We have known each other since we were children. Milko and I had made all of the arrangements for our marriage, but then he had to go into the Bulgarian army. Then the Nazis came, and he was taken to a concentration camp. Later, his parents received an official notice that he died in the camp. When I heard that Milko was dead, I came to Budapest. But yesterday came this letter from Milko and my mother. Milko was among the survivors returning to Bulgaria. He is very ill and needs me. So, you see, I must go back."

"Then why don't you tell Charley the truth?" I asked.

Leila pondered this for a moment. "No," she said, "once I heard a very old gypsy woman in my village say that we forget more quickly those we hate than we do those we love. When Charley reads this letter, he will hate me. I want him to forget me quickly."

"Well, what do you want me to do?"

"I want you to give the letter to Charley—tonight in the Apostles Bar, after the performance. I'm not strong enough to talk to Charley. I'm afraid to see him again. I'm afraid I wouldn't have the courage to leave."

So it was agreed, reluctantly on my part, that Charley and I would be in our usual seats at the theater that night. After the show, as was our custom, we would go to our booth at the Apostles and have a few drinks while waiting for Leila to join us. I placed the little white envelope in the inside pocket of my jacket.

"Wait for me there for one hour," Leila said, "then please give Charley the letter."

The theater was sold out that night; many people who could not get seats were standing. Charley and I went directly to our reserved seats in the center of the fifth row. There were several comic skits, in which Leila had minor roles, a few juggling acts, and a magician sawed a girl in half.

Leila was obviously the star and, after a lively Hungarian folk dance, the audience realized that it was closing time and began shouting for Leila. As always, she would close the show with two songs.

As the orchestra played a fanfare, the curtain parted, and the master of ceremonies walked to the microphone, holding up both hands in a vain attempt to halt the applause.

The audience, ignoring the signals from the stage for quiet, stood and applauded as Leila came from the wings and took her place before the microphone. She was wearing her beautiful parachute dress and seemed not to hear the applause nor to see the audience as she stood, unsmiling, with her hands clasped tightly in front of her bosom. It was cool in the theater, but I suddenly felt sweat on my neck.

The orchestra opened with the first few bars, and Leila sang *J'attendrai* in French, to the obvious delight of the audience. I impulsively felt for the envelope in my pocket. It was still there.

Without waiting for the applause to cease at the end of the song, Leila signaled the orchestra, and her rich contralto drifted smoothly into the lyrics of *Kiss Me Again*. The orchestra caught her mood and played a subdued background. She sang the words softly, almost as a lullaby. An enchanted hush settled upon the crowd in the theater.

> **Sweet summer breeze—whispering trees**
> **Stars shining softly above** . . .

I mopped the sweat from my forehead and looked at Charley from the corner of my eye. He was sitting very straight in his seat, smiling and proud as a peacock.

Leila turned her head slightly and looked directly at Charley. The spotlight reflected from the sequins on her dress— and from the tears which suddenly appeared on her cheeks.

Safe in your arms—far from alarms,
Daylight shall come—but in vain!

I loosened my tie and wished that I could be somewhere else—anywhere else. I looked at my watch. It was eleven.

Leila finished the song. There was complete silence in the theater for what seemed like several minutes before a storm of applause came from a standing audience. She bowed, threw a kiss to Charley, and the curtain closed.

The Apostles was almost empty as Charley and I went to our booth. We usually ordered beer, but this time I suggested that we start with a full bottle of strong Hungarian brandy. Charley was effusive in his praise of Leila's performance.

"What a voice she has!" he said. "She would be a star anywhere in the world!"

With a shaking hand, I poured Charley another double.

As the hour grew later, Charley began consulting his watch more often. "What's keeping her?" he moaned. "She's never been this late before."

When the hands on the Apostles' wall clock reached midnight, I poured one more brandy for Charley and placed a hand on his shoulder.

"Charley, I have bad news for you. Leila is not coming." I tried to keep my voice steady. "She has gone back to Bulgaria." I then told Charley the true story—just as Leila had told it to me that morning in my office.

At first, he seemed to be in a trance, and I knew it was not the brandy. As the shock wore off, tears came to his eyes. He began to ask questions. "How could you let her do this? She loves me! I know she loves me! Quick! Let's go to the railway station—we can stop her!"

It was all I could do to restrain him. Finishing the bottle of brandy helped. Even so, it was around three when we returned to the apartment.

As the weeks and months passed, Charley at last gave up hope of receiving a letter from Leila. His spirit was broken. At the end of the year he resigned from the Foreign Service and returned to California. I received two or three letters from him during the next five or ten years, as he drifted from job to job, before I finally lost touch. I heard from friends that he became an alcoholic. Charley never married.

The evening shadows lengthen in my study. The day is coming to an end. The pleasant voice on the record sings the final words of *Kiss Me Again*, and the stereo clicks off. As sounds of the village church bell float through my open window, I reach into a cranny of the old roll-top desk at my side and pull out a small envelope, once white but now yellowed. I don't open it, for I know well its contents.

As I pass the envelope through my fingers, I wonder what happened to Charley and to Leila. And I wonder if I made a mistake, not giving the letter to Charley, not doing it Leila's way.

THE TOUGHEST
CONSUL

THE TOUGHEST CONSUL

The old couple sat in the hall on the wooden bench just outside the American consul's office. They wore the Sunday-best garb of Hungarian peasants. His black trousers, clean but shiny from wear and patched at the knees, were tucked into a pair of black leather boots, highly polished but showing signs of age. The white shirt, which he wore buttoned at the throat without a tie, was covered by a countryman's typical black jacket with a neat patch on the sleeve. She wore several petticoats under a broad black skirt topped by a black jacket. Her gray hair was covered by a babushka scarf tied under her chin.

It was early in the day. The journey from their village in the country to Budapest had been arduous, and the strain was visible on their tanned wrinkled faces. They had arisen before sunrise to be certain of getting a train, since rail schedules were still not reliable following the recent end of

World War II. Unwrapping a small cloth bundle, he took out a piece of salami from which he cut several slices with his pocket knife. This was obviously their breakfast.

They had just finished the salami when Mrs. Keller, the vice consul's secretary, came out of her office to tell them, in Hungarian, that the visa section was further down the hall on the left. He wiped his gray moustache with his jacket sleeve. "But we American citizens," he said in English. "I'm Andy Szabo, and this here's Millie. Me and Millie don't need no visas. We come for American passport to go back to America. Here, I have American passport." Mrs. Keller took the old soiled, dog-eared document and said that since they were the first passport applicants of the day that the vice consul would see them in a few minutes. The old man patted Millie's hand gently. "You see, mama," he said softly, "nothing to worry about. We go back to America." She smiled and nodded.

An American consulate is an arcade through which passes almost every type of human being—the knights and the knaves, the saints and the sinners, and in Vice Consul Brannon's mind they were all sinners until proven otherwise.

Dirk Brannon, age thirty-seven, unmarried, began life in the old Hell's Kitchen section of New York City. He had been a stevedore on the city's docks as well as a professional boxer. He had come into the foreign service from the U. S. Marine Corps, where he had earned a chestfull of medals, which he never wore. He was six feet four inches tall, weighed two hundred and twenty pounds and had a cauliflower ear, a set of false teeth and a crew cut. His favorite amusement at parties, which he seldom attended, was tearing a New York telephone book, or similar document, crosswise in two parts with his bare hands. His normal speaking voice, even in the lower registers, sounded like heavy-duty truck tires skidding on a gravelled road. In a word, Vice Consul Brannon was tough—physically and mentally tough. While previously serving as shipping officer at various U. S. consulates in Latin American ports, he had gained the reputation among ship captains as the "toughest consul in the world." Any captain or sailor who ventured into his office in a drunken state risked being literally thrown out of the consulate or being severely beaten. Vice Consul Brannon never aspired to the career diplomatic service, since he was aware of a notation in his personnel records that he was "anti-social and prone to physical violence at the slightest provocation." When he became citizenship and passport officer at the consulate in Budapest after World War II, he was of the decided opinion that any American citizen who had remained in Hungary for the duration of the war had done so for only one reason—a belief that America would lose the war. Consequently, such persons could expect no sympathy from Vice Consul Brannon. Indeed, he took a special delight in personally informing such passport applicants that they had lost their claims to American citizenship if they had run afoul of the U. S. nationality laws—which was usually the case.

Mrs. Keller helped Andy and Millie fill in the required passport application forms and ushered them into Vice Consul Brannon's office. The vice consul, sitting behind a large table, in lieu of a normal desk, didn't say a word, he never wasted time by greeting applicants or employees. Mrs. Keller placed the documents, including the old passport, on the table while Andy and Millie stood more or less at attention, ignoring the two chairs before the table. "I am Andy Szabo. This here's Millie. We come for the American passport to go back to America."

Vice Consul Brannon studied the papers for a minute. "Sit!" he finally said. Mrs. Keller stood by ready to translate if necessary, since several of the documents which Andy presented were in Hungarian. "Andrew Szabo," Brannon said, finally looking directly at Andy and Millie sitting uneasily on the chairs, "both you and your wife were born in Hungary. Both of you were naturalized as American citizens in the United States. You lived there for many years. You both came back to Hungary in 1931 and have lived here since that time. We have no records here that you registered at the consulate as Americans or applied for renewal of your passports. Why did you come back to Hungary, Andy? There was no war on then."

Andy stood, holding his black hat before his waist. "Mr. Consul, sir, me and Millie come back here because we couldn't get no more work in America. You know, it was the hard times in 1931. No, we didn't think about a war then. Me and Millie had a good job with Mr. Sinclair out on Long Island. I was gardener and Millie was his cook. He had big house there and big family. Then, in 1931 in the big depression time, Mr. Sinclair he lost everything. I looked for other work, but there was nothing. Everybody out of work. My younger brother was farming the small piece of land here in Hungary that we had from our parents. We have a little house there. Me and Millie had to come back here to make a living. We worked here very hard, sir, and we made a pretty good living on the farm until the war come. About coming to the consulate for the register, sir, nobody never told us that we have to do that."

"Why do you want to go back to America now? Do you have any family there?" Brannon asked.

"No, sir. We got no children. We got nobody no more in America or here. It's just me and Millie now. My younger brother died in Russia during the war, and now the communists in our village say they going to take away the little farm and our house. We won't have no way to make a living here."

"But you and Millie are over seventy years old," Brannon said. "Do you have friends in America? Are you in touch with the Sinclair family?"

Andy's face brightened. He smiled, reached down and held Millie's hand. "No, sir," he said, we don't know nobody there, and I don't know what happened to Mr. Sinclair. Oh! what a fine man he was—and smart too! I'm sure he's back in business again, and me and Millie will go back and find him. He'll give us our jobs back again. He was always good to us." Millie smiled and nodded.

Vice Consul Brannon indicated the papers on the table. "What are these Hungarian documents, Mrs. Keller?"

Before Mrs. Keller could reply, Andy said, "Consul, sir, these are some papers me and Millie had to sign when we come back to our village. The mayor brought them over one day and said we would have to sign them if we wanted to stay in Hungary and work our farm. Later, some office here in Budapest sent us more papers that we had to swear to and sign. They all had something to do with our staying in the village. We never knew exactly what they are for, but you'll see there it says we Americans, and that there's our American passport. The whole village knows we are Americans—I think that's why the communists want to take our farm first."

Mrs. Keller picked up one of the documents and began to translate but, after a few words, found that she could not continue. She placed the document on the table and, in a choked voice, barely audible, said, "I'm sorry, Mr. Brannon. This is a declaration of allegiance to Hungary. They regained Hungarian citizenship. It is recorded in the ministry here in Budapest. They also voted in the Hungarian elections."

Mrs. Keller stood nervously waiting for Vice Consul Brannon to tell Andy and Millie in his usual brusque manner that they had lost their American citizenship. This was the moment that he always seemed to enjoy most, and she was always relieved when it was over. She could not understand the delay.

Vice Consul Brannon was silent for a while. He looked down at his shoes, stared at the chandelier. He even picked a few pieces of invisible lint from his jacket sleeve and loosened his shirt collar. Then he did a thing that was strange for him. He stood up, handed all of the papers to Mrs. Keller and said, "Mrs. Keller, take Andy and Millie to your office and explain the situation to them."

Vice Consul Brannon was standing alone in his office, hands clasped behind his back, gazing through a window when he saw Andy and Millie leaving the consulate. They were going slowly, still holding hands, across Victory Square in the direction of the railway station. They walked slightly stooped, as if their feet were too heavy for the long journey ahead.

"Mrs. Keller!" Brannon shouted, "tell the other applicants that they will have to wait awhile. I have some business to take care of in the visa section."

Vice Consul Brannon lied. He had no business to take care of in the visa section. Instead, he went to the men's room on the second floor and closed himself into one of the stalls. After all, it would never do to have the staff see tears on the cheeks of the world's toughest consul.

WITH NO
REGRETS

WITH NO REGRETS

"Did you bring the money?" Peter asked.

"Yes," I said, "but only half of it. You'll get the rest at the railway station when you meet the colonel. He'll give it to you himself."

It was late in the evening, and Peter and I were the only customers in the dreary little coffeehouse in the industrial section of Budapest. We sat in our overcoats and sipped tiny cups of black expresso coffee mixed with *barack palinka*, the fiery Hungarian plum brandy, as an antidote against the cool autumn weather. Well over a year had passed since the end of World War II, but Russian-occupied Budapest still suffered a shortage of heating fuel. Peter, which probably was not his real name, was a young Hungarian in his late twenties, and he was a smuggler. But Peter was no ordinary smuggler—he smuggled people without passports and visas out of Communist Hungary to freedom in Austria. He preferred to be called a guide.

"That's O.K.," he said. "You'll please excuse me that I have to charge so much, but I usually take three or four people each time. Since your colonel insists that he be the only one, I have to charge more. I also have to tell you that this will be my last trip. I'm staying on the other side this time—if we make it. It has become too dangerous. The Hungarian political and economic police have been asking questions about me. Winter will soon be here, and that also makes crossing the border a greater risk."

I was sorry to hear that Peter was giving up his business, since several of my Hungarian friends had successfully used his services. Good "guides" were difficult to find. Most of them were eventually caught by Soviet troops guarding the Hungarian border, or by Hungarian guards, and killed on the spot, or given long prison terms.

Peter placed the thick envelope in his pocket. "It's all set then. The colonel will be at the main Budapest railway station on Friday of next week at 12:30 p.m. He will have no suitcase, no knapsack—just the clothes that he wears. Nothing else. He will carry a rolled newspaper in his left hand. I will approach him and ask in English if he knows when the next train leaves for Debrecen. He will reply that he does not know, that he is waiting for his uncle to arrive from Warsaw. I will have two train tickets to Magyarovar. A car will pick us up there and take us to a farm near the Austrian border. We will begin the walk from there. Make certain he has sturdy shoes."

"Just one more thing, Peter," I said, as we finished the brandy and prepared to leave. "As I told you, this man is presumably a Soviet intelligence officer. He might be an *agent provocateur* who will try to alert the Russian or Hungarian border guards. Do you have a pistol or revolver?"

Peter was surprised. "Well, yes, I have a P-38 pistol at the farm, but I've never carried it. If the border guards catch me with it, I'll be shot immediately."

"Carry it with you this time, Peter, and if he tries any funny business, be sure that he is dead before you run away!"

Peter had an abiding hatred of communists in general and of Russians in particular. His sister had been raped by Russian soldiers and an older brother shipped to the Soviet Union for slave labor. I could trust him to carry out this request. "Then I suppose I'll not be seeing you again," I said. "Is there any way you can let me know if you make it across the border?"

"It may not be possible. My helpers at the farm are also going over next week. They're emigrating to Canada, and I'll probably go with them. You might check with your consulate in Vienna. They could tell you if the colonel shows up there. Of course, he might go to the American military headquarters in Vienna or even to the Austrian police. He could also go to the British or French consulates."

We shook hands, said good-bye, and I never saw or heard from Peter again.

There was a time shortly after World War II when there was some fraternization between the Russians and the Americans. True, even then these social contacts were limited, and it was unusual for a Soviet military officer or a Soviet diplomat to meet with an American without being accompanied by one or more other Russians. Thus when I met Ivan Povenko during my first year as an American consular officer in Budapest, he was in the company of other Soviet officials. He came to the Park Club one day, together with several people from the Soviet Kommandatura in Budapest, to attend a luncheon given by the American and British legations. He was in civilian clothes and was introduced to me simply as Mr. Povenko from the Soviet consulate. He was seated next to me at the table. He was a young man, about the same age as I, and spoke excellent English with a very British accent. He volunteered that he was unmarried and that he had served in London during the war. He was fluent in several languages and obviously extremely well educated, and he seemed to be interested in everything American. It developed that he was an ardent fisherman, as was I, and I invited him to accompany me the following weekend to a well known trout lake. Much to my surprise, he accepted—of course with a proviso that he could bring a friend.

We spent an enjoyable fishing weekend at Lillafured. The friend, whom he introduced as Captain Nikolai, wore a Soviet army uniform and spoke only Russian, although I suspected that he understood English. Nikolai was not a fisherman, but he accompanied us each time we went to the lake. He refused, however, to get into the rowboat with us. The poor fellow was prone to seasickness and sat on the bank with a few bottles of beer.

Povenko and I fished together almost every weekend that spring and summer and came to know each other well. He was an excellent fly angler and taught me many new ways of casting for trout. While we were in the rowboat— with Nikolai sitting happily under a tree with his beer— Povenko would talk of his childhood in the Soviet Union. His brother, the only living member of his family, worked in a factory in Leningrad. His parents had been killed during the war. He had been selected by his government for training in a "special school" because he excelled in foreign languages.

One day near the end of summer, when the fishing season was almost over, Povenko and I were sitting in our rowboat still trying for the "big one." He reeled in his line and rested the rod on the bottom of the boat. "I wonder if you would do me a favor," he said suddenly, looking quickly over both shoulders as if he thought someone else might be listening.

"Of course," I replied, "if I can."

He took a deep breath, as a swimmer does before diving into a cold pool. "I want to go to the United States—to live and work there. I want to become a United States citizen. I wanted to defect when I was in London, but I didn't have a chance to break away from the others in my organization. I haven't been entirely truthful with you, for reasons which you might understand. I work directly with the People's Commissariat for Internal Affairs in Moscow. You know it, I believe, as the N.K.V.D. I hold the rank of colonel, and I have information which will be of value to your intelligence services. I am willing to give them this information if they will take me to the United States. Will you speak to someone in your legation about this? I realize that you would probably not risk flying me out from Hungary and that I will have to cross the border to Austria on my own, but even with this I would want your help. The guides I know are working for the Soviet Kommandatura, and it would be suicide for me to trust them."

I tried hard, but unsuccessfully, not to show my surprise. "All right. I'll make inquiries and try to have news for you next weekend." We rowed back to shore and helped Nikolai finish his beer.

Early the next morning, I repeated Colonel Povenko's request to my superiors. The unanimous decision was that he would have to go to Austria and make his request to the American consulate or to the American military command in Vienna. We would alert the consulate in Vienna, but we could offer no encouragement nor could we officially assist him to cross the Austrian border. So far as we were concerned, he was a Soviet *agent provocateur*.

Colonel Povenko and I had no real interest in fishing

when we rowed to the center of the lake the following Saturday afternoon. The fish were not biting anyway. Nikolai sat under his tree as usual. Povenko was pleased with my report, since he had not expected more. I told him that I had, unofficially, talked with a guide, known to me to be reliable, and that he wanted one thousand U.S. dollars in cash to take him over the border—five hundred which I would have to give the guide before they met to begin the trip. I also requested a passport photo, which I would send to the American consulate in Vienna. To my amazement, he took out his wallet and handed me a photo and five one-hundred dollar bills.

After my rendezvous in the coffeehouse with Peter, Colonel Povenko and I met for the last time at an official dinner party the following Wednesday at the luxurious Park Club in Budapest. It was a gala event sponsored by the American and British legations. There was music, dancing, and the food and champagne were plentiful. High-ranking officers of the Soviet military and consulate in Budapest were guests, and I managed to be seated next to Povenko. While the tables were being cleared for dessert, I gave the colonel a prearranged signal, excused myself and went to the men's room. He joined me there a few minutes later, and when we were alone, I handed him a brief, typed list of Peter's instructions and told him that I had paid the five hundred dollars. He read the list hurriedly.

"That's day after tomorrow," I said. "Not much time left. Can you make it?"

I thought I saw tears in the colonel's eyes. "I've waited many years for this moment. Yes, I can make it. Thank you. I hope we can be in touch again, but I doubt it. From what I know of your people, if I make it to the United States, they will give me a new name, a new identity. My past will be buried forever."

I'll never really know why I did it—it was an impulsive

thing. I quickly took from my vest pocket a small, gold plated medal of Saint Christopher, the patron saint of travelers, and put it in his hand. "Take this," I told him. "You'll need all the help you can get. Good-bye, good luck, and I hope you will have no regrets."

He smiled and pocketed the little medal. "No. No regrets," he said.

During the next several weeks, I religiously searched the Hungarian and Austrian newspapers for news of border incidents. I found nothing. I repeatedly asked friends who dealt with such matters at the consulate in Vienna whether the colonel had come in. The reply was always negative. Both Peter and Colonel Povenko had disappeared without a trace.

The years passed, bringing new posts in other parts of the world, different jobs and, finally, retirement. For many years I would occasionally think of the colonel, especially when alone on a trout stream or in the middle of a lake trying for the "big one." But I must confess that time eventually erased him from my mind.

It was a beautiful August day in the foothills of the Black Forest of Southern Germany. My wife and I were cutting a few roses from the small garden of our retirement cottage when the postman from the village brought a registered letter. At our age, a registered letter usually brings unpleasant news, and we opened it with some trepidation, the more so since the return address was that of a well known medical research organization in the United States. The letter was signed by one of the internationally most prestigious names in the medical profession:

Dear Sir:
My father, Professor _____, former head of the Slavic Languages Department of _____ University, passed away on June sixteenth after

suffering a stroke. Upon opening his safe, we found an envelope bearing your name, along with a note in my father's handwriting stating that we should get your address from the State Department in Washington, D. C. and send the envelope to you. It is enclosed herewith.

My father immigrated to the United States shortly after World II from Yugoslavia. He got a teaching job at the University of _____ , where he met and married my mother, who died last year. He brought no family records with him, and he never spoke of his life and family in Yugoslavia. It occurs to us that you probably knew him in Yugoslavia, and I would be very interested to hear from you in this regard. My sister and I would be most grateful for any family information you could provide.

Sincerely,

_____ , M. D.

The enclosed unsealed envelope contained a small, worn Saint Christopher medal and a slip of paper on which was written just two words, "No Regrets."

It would have been a great honor for me to correspond with Dr. _____ , but I never answered his letter. I prefer to let my old fishing companion rest in peace—with no regrets.

RETIREMENT DAY

RETIREMENT DAY

Sit over here in the easy chair. It has a few broken springs, but it's the only comfortable one in the office. I don't have many visitors. I'll pour you a small brandy against the cold while I put a few things in this suitcase. It will only take a few minutes.

Yesterday was officially my last day in the office. It's hard to believe that retirement day has finally caught up with me. Where did all of those years go? Like water through a sieve. I came in this morning only to clean out my desk, pack a few things, and say a final goodbye to the local staff with whom I've worked so well for the past year. I hate saying good-byes, even though they are a large part of life in the foreign service. "Comes with the territory," they say, but I never got used to it, especially with the local staff. With fellow American employees it was different. There was always a chance that you would run into them in Washington or at some other post. With the locals, you realize that you will probably never see any of them again.

Cards have been sent to all of my diplomatic colleagues, as required by protocol. My bills have been paid, the apartment closed, and Pipi, the cat, given to a neighbor who promised not to have him castrated. The going-away parties are all finished. There's been one every night for the past week, but the one at the ambassador's last night was a real killer. I'm still not feeling too steady. Here, have a look at this. It's a silver cigar box with my initials on the lid (I don't smoke). It was given to me last night by the ambassador, and this silver tea pot (I don't drink tea) with my initials on the side is from the local staff. The ambassador made a very nice little speech, even said, not very convincingly, that he envied me and promised to visit me and my wife sometime at our retirement home in Florida.

See that photo there on the desk—the one in the silver frame? That's Margaret. It was taken in Barranquilla, Colombia, my first post as a young vice consul. She was 25 and, as you will note, very pretty. I was 26, and we had just been married. We were both fresh out of the university and very much in love. Seems only yesterday.

Margaret didn't come with me to this post. I had only one more year to serve before retirement, so she remained in Gainesville to supervise some repairs to the small house we bought there several years ago. Here, this is a picture of the house. That's Margaret standing in the garden. I planted all of those flowers myself. See the little water fountain there? I built it with my own hands. We decided to retire there to be near our son, Tony, who is now a professor at the University of Florida. Over the years I finally managed to save enough to pay off the mortgage and build up a nice little bank account. Margaret and I reckoned that we would both still be relatively young when I retired and that I would be able to get a teaching job at the university, and she would open a small shop of some sort.

This picture here, in the wooden frame, is of our son. It was taken when he was five years old. He was born in Vienna, and we almost lost him a couple of times. The first was at his birth, shortly after World War II. The baby got an infection at the hospital and almost died. I managed to get the hospital some penicillin—which was in short supply—and his life was saved.

Another time, in Jakarta, Tony came down with some kind of fever. There was only one western-trained doctor on the island of Java at the time—an Italian—and he was sick and unable to help us. We called in a local Chinese herb doctor and prayed. It took a month, but Tony recovered.

Shortly after the boy's recovery from this illness, I noticed a subtle change in Margaret. It was nothing that I could define exactly, but it was as if she had lost all interest in her surroundings and current events. She even began to neglect the boy, leaving his care almost entirely to an Indonesian nurse. One day she suggested that things might be better if we resigned from the Service and returned to the States. She also began to drink heavily.

The transfer to London came just at the right time and was apparently good for Margaret. She stopped the heavy drinking, took a greater interest in the boy, joined a club, and seemed happy in the English-speaking environment. But just when I thought things were returning to normal, I learned she was having an affair with an employee of the French embassy. Most everyone in the diplomatic community knew about it; and now I know that it hindered my career. To stop the affair, I arranged for Margaret and Tony to return to her mother in North Carolina for an extended visit.

After London came more of the "less attractive" posts,

where my family rejoined me. Sometimes living conditions for us were harsh, even dangerous, but Margaret busied herself with Tony's education and local charity organizations, and we lived a more or less normal life. Oh, there were other little affairs that Margaret thought she kept hidden, but the diplomatic colony is usually aware of such things: the tennis instructor in Singapore; the U. N. scientist and the Australian businessman in Rangoon; the horse trainer in Mexico City. For Tony's sake I did everything I could to keep our marriage intact and hoped that Margaret would finally come to her senses.

We grew older; with my promotions came better posts in Europe. Tony went to a boarding school in Massachusetts and later studied at the University of Pennsylvania, where he earned a degree. He spent the summers with us in Europe and the holidays with his grandparents in North Carolina. There were no more open scandals involving Margaret, and I began to look forward to a happy retirement with her in Florida—until six months ago.

The first disquieting letter I received was from the vice president of our bank in Gainesville. The bank was supposed to send all canceled checks to Margaret at our retirement address, but since the vice president is my old friend and a former classmate, he took the liberty of mailing me a stack of canceled checks, along with a very informative letter. The letter said our joint savings account had been changed by Margaret to a checking account, which was dangerously low. The canceled checks were even more ominous. Most of them were for cash—in large amounts— and others were made out to plush hotels in New York, Miami, Palm Springs, and San Francisco. There were still more, made out to various airlines.

But it was the second letter, from an old friend and retired foreign service officer living in Miami, that put the icing on the cake. He reported having seen Margaret with "a very handsome man who looked like a gigolo", at various times, in several Miami night clubs.

And then there's this letter. It came last week from my lawyer. He says he now has all of the necessary evidence constituting grounds for divorce, and that he will file my petition next week. I'm giving Margaret the house in Gainesville and, of course, she'll also get a part of my foreign service pension.

What about me? Well, as you can see, I'm packing my bags now. They will be shipped to me at the Chateau Sablonne in a small village near Paris. The Countess de Sablonne is waiting for me outside in the Rolls. We will drive from here to the Riviera and spend the rest of the winter in her villa in the hills above Cannes. As soon as my divorce is final, we will be married there, then return to the chateau for the summer, where I will busy myself learning viniculture and other aspects of the wine business. Incidentally, that's a photo of the countess there—the one with the gold frame.

EPILOGUE

LEST I FORGET: NOTES FROM A CAPTIVE LAND

EPILOGUE

LEST I FORGET:
NOTES FROM A CAPTIVE LAND

Years ago, I promised some friends that, one day, I would write a book. I last made this careless statement to a man in the employ of the Communist secret police in Budapest, Hungary, which for almost five years, 1945-1950, was my post in the Foreign Service of the United States.

As I read these lines, this seems a bit incredible; but, as I remember, there was nothing unusual about it that rainy October evening in 1949 as I sat across a tiny table from Professor Janos Bognar, Hungarian citizen, in a dreary little Budapest coffee house on Erzsebet Korut. It was not unusual to me then because Janos Bognar (which obviously isn't his real name) and his wife had been my friends in Hungary for several years—even before he was forced by threats against the lives of his family to enter the service of the Communist secret police as an informer. At considerable risk to his personal safety, he had told me of these circumstances at the beginning of his service with the Communists and warned me that he was required to make regular reports to the Communist political police of his conversations with me or other Americans in Hungary.

Our meeting that evening was, however, a memorable one, because it was to be our last. I recall the weariness of his face and the somber note in his voice as he cautiously, but calmly, told me that he and his wife had reached the limit which their tortured nerves could bear, and that they had decided to "go out black," a common Hungarian expression meaning that they would try to escape across the Hungarian border to the West without benefit of passports and visas.

Even as we talked over our cups of expresso black coffee, his wife was at their apartment packing the knapsacks for the journey.

So it was he, as we shook hands for the last time, who suggested that "someday, when the change comes" I should write a book and promised, jokingly, that I would have at least one reader, implying with typical Magyar humor that perhaps he would even go so far as to pay for his copy. He desperately wanted the people on the outside to know Hungary's terrible story.

Janos Bognar and his wife left Budapest that night. They never reached their destination in Vienna, and I never saw them again.

As my small tribute to Janos Bognar and to the touching courage and stamina of the thousands of other Janos Bognars trapped and enslaved in the Hungarian "People's Democracy," I feel that I should jot down some notes of what I have seen and experienced there.

Accordingly, I place these notes on record against the ravages of new hours and new places—lest I forget.

From Naples to Budapest

The ship which took me into Naples, Italy, that hot, humid day in June 1945 was the SS *Argentina* which was being used to bring home our military personnel from Italy. The Naples docks were nothing but rubble, and even Capri's war scars were clearly visible. I was less impressed by the beauty of the bay when the ship's captain told me that we would be several hours late getting to the dock in order to keep the ship away from floating mines.

My orders were to leave Naples as soon as plane transportation was available to join the United States State Department group which had been flown into Hungary several weeks before. This group was referred to in my orders as the "Hungarian Team." It was headed by the late United States Minister H. F. Arthur Schoenfeld. General William Key of Oklahoma was the U. S. Representative on the Allied Control Commission for Hungary. General Edgecomb represented Britain.

The flight from Naples to Budapest across Yugoslavia was a matter of a few hours. I wondered about the landing fields in Hungary since I had heard in Naples that the Red Army was occupying all of them. I didn't have long to think about it, as we were soon over the battered city of Budapest.

It was a clear, sunny day, and I shall always remember that first glimpse of post-war Budapest. I could see from the air that the damage had been great. As we approached the Danube I saw the rear section of a plane protruding from the top floor of a large building in Buda. The swastika on its tail was clearly visible. It had crashed headlong into the side of the building. The Danube bridges connecting the ancient city of Pest with mountainous Buda had been destroyed. I saw only one pontoon bridge. There seemed to be thousands of houses in Pest without roofs.

I soon learned that the Budapest airfield was in perfect condition, but that the Russian occupation forces would not permit their American and British allies to use it— hence, the cow pasture for us.

An American army car met us at the "field," and we drove about five miles to the city over roads and streets pock-marked by shells. Unexploded bombs and grenades were abundant along the roadside, and Russian troops were everywhere on the streets of Budapest.

Post War Budapest

This was July, 1945. Our Mission was known officially as the American Representation on the Allied Control Commission for Hungary. The Russians, whose troops had occupied Hungary, were in control of the Commission from the beginning and the minor roles to which the United States and Britain were relegated on the Commission became apparent later.

My first stop was at the American Mission building on Szabadsag ter (Victory Square) in the heart of Budapest, from where I was taken, together with my duffel bag and footlocker, to an apartment at Number 20, Bathory utca (street) which was to be my home for several exciting months. The four-room apartment was already occupied by three members of the Mission staff, Ernie Sharpe of Texas, Dave Pearsall of New York, and Bob Folsom of Florida. We were later joined by Dick Wood of New York and Lewis Revey of Ohio.

There were several pieces of ornate furniture but not enough beds for all of us; so, being the newcomer, I fell heir to the back of a shell-shocked sofa, which, when placed on the floor and covered with an army blanket, made a fairly comfortable bed. What our one stove lacked in practical utility, it made up in beauty. It was of polished clay slabs, browned by years of use to the color of an old meerschaum.

Some of the shops were open, and there was a small supply of vegetables and fruit. The population of Hungary, even in the city of Budapest, had used every available piece of ground for growing vegetables. On many front lawns in Budapest, corn and cabbages were growing on the new graves of German and Russian soldiers.

Merchants, including those just returned from Nazi concentration camps, were reopening their small textile shops stocked with clothing material which had been buried underground during the siege. Old window curtains and drapes were transformed into dresses by Budapest women. There were, however, shortages of fats and oils, and obtaining meat and flour was very difficult for the average Hungarian in Budapest.

Practically all of the automotive vehicles, as well as the horse and ox-drawn wagons in Hungary in 1945 belonged to the military. As the war approached, a few clever Hungarians had hidden their autos under haystacks in the fields— only to have them discovered when the Russians took the hay for their animals and bedding.

Several bars, night spots and many expressos (coffee houses) were already open in Budapest in July 1945. In fact, one Hungarian friend told me that as soon as the last shell had been fired and he had dared to come out of his air-raid shelter, he had strolled down Vaci utca, the Fifth Avenue of Budapest, and had a black coffee at an expresso. His story is, of course, doubtful; but in most of the expressos which were open when I arrived in Budapest, one could get real coffee.

One enterprising aristocrat set up a bar in one room of his apartment near Vaci utca, moved in a piano and began selling the stock from the family cellar, which had, some-how, been overlooked by the Russian troops.

The GIs, in Hungary as part of the United States Repre-sentation on the Allied Control Commission, were billeted in the Hotel Astoria in Budapest. They had their own club in the hotel basement called the Pengo Club—so named in honor of the pre-war monetary unit of Hungary.

The plush Park Club, on Stefania Street (now called Voroshilov Street) was reopened after the siege of Buda-pest as an "Allied Officers' Park Club." It had the pre-war reputation of being the most elite of European aristocratic clubs. Under the terms of the Armistice Agreement with Hungary, no charge was to be made for food, drink and service at the club to its members and their guests. It was supplied and operated by the Hungarian Government. In line with the United States decision not to exact reparations from Hungary, the American members did, however, pay for their food, drink and service at the club through the purchase of chit books.

Upon its reopening, the British and American members attempted to make the Park Club a truly "allied" organiza-tion by inviting the Russian officials of the Control Commis-sion to become members and take part in all of the club activities. The Russians always graciously accepted these invitations but never participated, and only their very high ranking officers came as guests on very official occasions.

The reopened Park Club retained every vestige of its past glory. Gypsy bands played there nightly, and Hungary's foremost stars of theater and opera performed there each week. Its red-carpeted halls were often trod by internation-ally famous personages. Alben Barkley headed one group of congressmen and senators which was entertained there, and it was in the Club's flower-filled garden that Matyas

Rakosi, the Communist Dictator of Hungary, Soviet Ambassador Pushkin, Zoltan Tildy, Ference Nagy and other Hungarian leaders attended a July 4th celebration given by the American Representative on the Allied Control Commission. This was the only time I ever spoke with Rakosi, who spoke excellent English. I remember wondering, as we exchanged pleasantries, how such a mild little man could be such a vicious enemy of our way of life. Later events were to prove the extent of his hatred for America. I also remember how strangely similar he appeared to old photographs I had seen of Bela Kun, Hungary's bloody Communist dictator who controlled the country for a few months after World War I.

Russian soldiers in Budapest were looting, robbing, raping and murdering nightly during the winter of 1945. Hungarian families in Budapest as well as in the villages lived in constant terror of roving bands of looting Russian soldiers. A curfew was in force for many months after the "liberation" of Budapest from the Germans; however, this curfew was not necessary to keep Hungarians off the streets after dark. They knew only too well the risks of venturing onto the street at night. There were no street lights in Budapest during the summer of 1945, and only a few were turned on by the end of that year.

Russian military police patrols were extremely ineffective at coping with the looting and robberies by their troops. These patrols were more inclined to assist their comrades in their nefarious activities than to arrest them, and it was not uncommon for drunken Russian military police patrols to fight pitched machine gun battles among themselves in Budapest streets.

We occupants of Number 20 Bathory Street were awakened almost nightly during the winter of 1945 by gunfire outside the doorway. Several mornings, as I left for my office, I stepped over the bodies of Russian soldiers near our doorway where they had been shot during the night.

The Hungarians excel in the arts. The magnificent Budapest opera house and a few variety theaters were reopened in 1945. Performances began early so that both audience and performers could be home before late evening to avoid being robbed on the streets by Russian soldiers.

I recall attending, together with an interpreter, a performance in the winter of 1945 at a small variety theater just around the corner from the Arizona club in Budapest. The leading actress wore an elaborate gown made from an abandoned American parachute, and the leading man had just returned to Budapest from a Nazi concentration camp in Germany. One of the soloists, however, received a deafening ovation for his rendition of a song about "when springtime comes again."

I left the theater that evening with a feeling for the first time of pity for that small audience of average Hungarians who actually believed that they would be able to begin a normal way of life when the springtime came again to their country.

Our American Consulate was reopened in the summer of 1945 at Szabadsag ter (Victory Square) Number 12. The building overlooked a large square in the approximate center of the business district of Budapest on the Pest side of the Danube.

In addition to a huge Russian monument to Russia's war dead, the square contained a figure in bronze of a nude woman with uplifted arms and minus her right breast which was shot away during the battle for Budapest in 1944. In the center of the square was a bronze statue of General Bandholtz, the American General who represented the United

States on the Allied Control Commission in Hungary after World War I. Both were removed by the Communists to make more space for the people forced to gather in the square to pay homage to the Soviet Union on Red Army holidays and other Communist festive occasions.

Immediately after its opening, the Consulate was swamped by requests from Americans and Hungarians in the United States for information as to the whereabouts and welfare of long-missing relatives and friends.

Hundreds of American citizens and persons claiming American citizenship flocked to the Consulate every day, and we were screening these applicants and issuing American passports before the winter of 1945. I soon found all of my time devoted to this work and was placed in charge of the Citizenship, Passport and Repatriation Branch of our Consulate. My job was to interview applicants for American passports, determine their citizenship claims and get them to the United States—or to other countries in cases where they were citizens of a country represented by the United States. We repatriated several citizens of various Latin American countries and the Philippines who had been stranded in Hungary during the war.

The winter of 1945 was one of continued suffering for Hungary. The severe cold caught Budapest and most of the battle-torn villages without proper housing and with practically no fuel. The fuel delivery system of the United States Mission broke down, and the Consulate building was without any form of heat for several months. It was, however, business as usual at the Consulate, and we sat at our desks in heavy overcoats. I supplemented the coat with an army blanket wrapped around my feet until one day when I decided to transfer the Citizenship Section of the Consulate to the apartment at Number 20 Bathory Street. There I interviewed applicants for several days in the luxurious warmth of our beautiful stove. I removed my office to the Consulate building upon the arrival of a truck load of coal.

The majority of our United States citizen applicants for repatriation were loyal Americans who had simply waited too long to heed warnings of the United States Consulate General in Budapest before the outbreak of World War II to quit the country. There were a few, however, who told me frankly that they had remained in Hungary because they had felt certain that the United States and her allies would lose the war. They were American citizens. Many of them, however, were never able to realize their post-war dreams of returning to the United States as it was found that they had committed certain acts causing the loss of their United States nationality.

Several persons appeared at the Consulate with old, mutilated American passports from which the photographs had been removed and falsely represented themselves to be the persons to whom the passports had been issued. These imposters were quickly found out by a check of old dossiers.

A large number of American citizens were killed in Budapest when the Festetich utca camp where they were interned by the Hungarians received a direct bomb hit from an unidentified plane in 1944. Many more were machine gunned by the Nazis on the banks of the Danube. There were also American citizens among the thousands of persons deported to Hitler's death camps from Hungary.

The American Consulate spared no effort to locate any person in Hungary who had a claim to American citizenship. It was one of these efforts which caused John Morgan, another Vice Consul, and me to be arrested by the Russian military in Hungary in 1946. Morgan, subsequently decorated by the U. S. State Department for his work in Russia as a member of the American Consular Staff during the war, was returning to Budapest with me by jeep one summer day after a trip into the country. We had visited several small villages near Miskolc, where we had been searching for details regarding the deportation of an American citizen from Hungary to Russia. We had obtained some information about the case, and I had a few notes about it in my pocket. We were bouncing happily along in our jeep when, about ten miles from the small village of Szikszo, near Miskolc, I saw a big rabbit run into a nearby wheat field. We stopped on the roadside and, taking our rabbit gun, gave chase. We didn't get the rabbit, and when we returned to our jeep we found it surrounded by twelve Russian soldiers under the command of a colonel. The "allies" had their tommy-guns trained on us as the colonel asked us what we were doing there. Morgan, who spoke excellent Russian, answered that we were "hunting rabbits," whereupon the colonel made the surprising statement that we had no right to be there. We replied that we Americans were also members of the Control Commission for Hungary.

The conversation finally ended with the colonel ordering us to follow his jeep to the Russian Kommandatura, or military headquarters in Szikszo. To insure our compliance, another jeep filled with armed Russians followed us.

The narrow road was very dusty, so while Morgan drove as fast as possible to make a dust screen, I took the notes from my pocket, tore them to bits and scattered them along the roadway. We knew that we would be searched upon arrival at the Kommandatura.

Upon arriving at Szikszo we were made to park our jeep in the courtyard of a large building which served as the Red

Army Kommandatura, and were escorted to an upstairs room. There the Russian colonel again began questioning us as to our reasons for being in that area. He invariably received the same reply—"rabbit hunting." We were kept in the Kommandatura for about 12 hours, during which time we received some raw bacon, some half-cooked potatoes and straight Hungarian rum.

Our subsequent release was probably aided by a young lieutenant there who had a sister in Cleveland. Our jeep was returned to us and we set out again for Budapest. We didn't look for any more rabbits from Szikszo to Budapest.

My jeep excursions into the Hungarian countryside often brought me in touch with other Red Army Kommandaturas, but fortunately under more friendly circumstances.

The Russians had divided Hungary into military districts headed by Kommandaturas. These were usually in charge of a major or captain, depending on the size or importance of the district. I never saw a Russian soldier in the small villages or the country who was not accompanied by several or at least one other Russian soldier, and I never saw one who was not armed to the teeth. I never quite knew whether they had a great fear of loneliness or of the Hungarian peasants.

I met several Russian army officers in Hungary who were very hospitable—but who never dared accept American hospitality in return. One of these was a Red Army major in command of the Kommandatura at the small village of Paks, on the Danube about forty miles from Budapest. The major and most of his staff had been among the Russian troops who had met the Americans at the Elbe at the finish of the war in Germany. He often boasted to me about the large numbers of pigs, chickens and beef cattle his men had "requisitioned" from the Hungarian countryside. When I suggested that perhaps he was taking more than his men needed, he replied, "the Magyars are too rich—they can spare it." Indeed, this seems to be the philosophy of Moscow even to the present day.

Not all of the items "requisitioned" by the Soviet occupation forces in Hungary were for the immediate use of the troops, and not all of the material taken was for food. I have seen many trains from Hungary en route to the Soviet Union before and after the signing of the Peace Treaty, loaded with such items as bath tubs, commodes, toilet seats and ordinary wooden window frames (without glass). Many trains left for the Soviet Union carrying carloads of sailboats and small rowboats from Lake Balaton. It was common practice for Hungarians to offer their Balaton sailboats to the American or British diplomatic personnel in Hungary to keep the boats from being taken away by the Russians.

There is hardly a village in Hungary that has not had a part of its civilian population abducted for forced labor in Russia. This includes both men and women. Many persons having a claim to American citizenship were forcibly taken from Hungary to Russia by the Red Army, and most of the efforts of American authorities to obtain their release were in vain.

Abductions began as soon as the Red Army entered Hungary, and Hungarians lived in mortal terror of the knock on the door at night which could have meant spending their remaining days laboring in the Soviet Union.

On many occasions, Hungarian citizens came into the consulate in Budapest and requested permission to stay in the building overnight or for several days to avoid arrest and deportation to Russia. The Consulate, of course, was not permitted to grant these requests for sanctuary. One man had a nervous breakdown in my office when informed that our government could not permit him to hide in the

Consulate building from the Hungarian-Russian secret police. His crime was that he had refused to become an informer for the Communist police against his friends.

April 30, 1945, is usually regarded as the beginning of the great post-war inflation in Hungary which was to reach such proportions that a briefcase full of Hungarian notes would not buy a sandwich.

A rapid rise in general prices accompanied a heavy expansion of note circulation, and soon gold and dollars became the only real standard in Hungary. Most Hungarian families in Budapest, during the early months of 1946, were living from day to day by exchanging a small piece of broken gold or jewelry for food and clothing. I had one Hungarian friend who was living at that time from a gold watch chain— he sold one link of the chain every four days.

These were also the days of the *ado pengo* or "tax money," introduced on January 1, 1946. The *ado pengo* was a special paper currency designed for paying taxes— necessitated by the fact that tax payments lost practically all of their real value during the period between assessment and payment. The value of this tax currency was fixed from day to day by the government. It was also used in credit transactions, and the Central Bank of Hungary only discounted bills of exchange drawn in the *ado pengo*. Since the *ado pengo* was a little slower to lose its value than the regular currency, there was a daily rush by everyone to exchange the regular currency for the tax money. Finally, however, the tax money became almost as worthless as the pengo notes.

Hungary's new currency, the florin, or forint, was introduced on August 1, 1946 and was linked with gold in the ratio of 1 kilogram of fine gold equaled 13,210 forints. One forint was equal to 400,000 quadrillion pengos or 200,000 million *ado pengos*.

It is a time-honored function of American Consulates to attempt to obtain protection for United States citizens. The Consulate in Budapest was able to obtain a reasonable degree of cooperation in this respect from the Hungarian Government until 1947. The Hungarian police were very cooperative with the consular officials in aiding American citizens for the first year and a half after the war, and the various precinct stations were always alert in those days to aid an American citizen in distress. This alertness on their part involved me in the case of the "American Girl-Soldier."

One spring day in 1946, I received a frantic telephone call from a precinct police captain in Buda. He told me politely that he was indeed very sorry, but it had been necessary for one of his men to arrest "an American Girl-Soldier" on charges of theft, drunkenness and disorderly conduct, and would I kindly send someone out to his police station to take her away. I most assuredly would. I knew that an "American Girl-Soldier" could mean only one thing: A WAC—and I knew that we had no WACs in Hungary. The mystery grew deeper as one of the Hungarian employees of the Consulate and I sped to Buda in our jeep.

We entered the police station, and I asked the captain where the "girl-soldier" had come from and how he knew that she was an American. He replied that she had come into Budapest from Germany, that she spoke English (which the captain didn't speak) and was dressed in an American army uniform with the American flag on her sleeve. He added that she also spoke Rumanian, which he understood.

Without further delay he brought out the prisoner—a plump young lady dressed partly in the uniform of an American WAC and obviously in the last stages of a tremendous binge.

"Do you speak English?" I asked.

Her reply may never appear in the history books along with expressions like "Remember the Alamo" or "Lafayette, we are here," but it will be there just the same in the memory of every American GI who ever set foot on European soil. She turned to me with a broad smile.

"Me spik English," she said. "Allo, Baby! You gottee cigaret?"

The severe winter of 1945 and the shortage of fuel and clothing in Hungary gave rise to an unusual form of robbery known to the police as "stripping." Roving stick-up men would attack persons on the streets at night and strip them of every article of clothing which they were wearing.

One such attempted robbery resulted in the murder of an American citizen who had returned to Budapest shortly after the war to visit relatives. He was accosted one evening on Stefania Street in Budapest by several persons in Russian army uniforms and speaking Russian. When he refused to take off his overcoat, he was killed by a burst of tommygun fire. Before he died, he described his attackers as Russian soldiers.

The Hungarian criminal police, which at that time were not completely dominated by Communists, were powerless in their efforts to trace the murderer because none of the Russian army officials in Hungary would give them any information or assistance.

There were several American students at Hungarian universities who were trapped there by the war. Most of them were medical students at Pecs. When the Consulate began functioning, arrangements were made to repatriate them to the United States, and I repeatedly urged each of them to return to the United States as soon as possible. One of them, however, had only a few months' work to do before receiving his degree, and he decided to remain in Hungary a few months for this purpose. Soon one of his colleagues came to the Consulate with news that he had been abducted by Russian soldiers.

Through reliable sources, I learned that he was being held prisoner in the basement of a Russian Kommandatura at Debrecen, Hungary, and accompanied by Colonel Peter Kopcsak of the American army (Colonel Kopcsak was later expelled from Hungary by the Communists), I proceeded to Debrecen to attempt to have him released. Thinking that it would be easier to secure his release through the Hungarian police, we went first to the Hungarian police chief in Debrecen. I soon found that he was a fanatical Communist who was reluctant to answer any questions. Nevertheless, I gave him the last name of the student and asked him whether the Hungarians were holding him prisoner.

"How do you expect us to know whether we have this man as a prisoner without giving us his first name," was his reply.

He was obviously embarrassed when I expressed amazement to learn that the Hungarians were holding so many persons with that name in their prison in Debrecen.

We then went to see the Russian major in charge of the Kommandatura where we knew the prisoner was being held. He blandly denied having the boy there and refused to permit us to go through the Kommandatura building.

All of our extended efforts to obtain the release of this student were in vain.

It has been written that the peasants are the backbone of Hungary. During my years in Hungary, I became very well acquainted with these peasant farmers. I found them to be resourcetul, shrewd, honest, religious, superstitious, and very industrious.

The Hungarian peasant has become accustomed, through the centuries, to tyranny of one form or another, but his taste of communism, coming so soon after his plunder by the Red Army, has left him extremely bitter toward everything Russian. Many peasant families have told me that they would welcome the Nazis again in preference to the Communists. This is, perhaps, because the Communists have come closer than any of the tyrants to taking away the implements of their existence.

A great number of peasant families had sons or fathers murdered by the Russians and the Communists, and even greater numbers had daughters or mothers violated by Russian troops. I have had more than several peasant boys tell me, while out on a hunt, how they would deal with the Communists and the Russians if the opportunity should come. These are the same peasant youths who are being forced to serve in the Russian-controlled Hungarian Army.

Hungary went to the polls in 1945 to vote in the only fair, honest elections which have been held in the country since the war. As the world soon learned, the decisive victory in those elections for the anti-Communist Smallholders Party (so called because it represented primarily the small land farmers) did not loosen the tightening grip of Russia. The anti-Communist parties were forced by Soviet pressure to give the most important governmental posts, including the Ministry of Interior, to Communists. This, to a large extent, nullified the Smallholders victory at the polls.

I shall always remember one event in particular which took place in Budapest during the election campaign. Early one afternoon, I was startled by a roar of voices outside the

Consulate windows. Together with the other consular employees, I ran to a large window facing the Szabadsag Square. The square was literally packed with shouting, singing people. Some of them carried huge signs reading "Long Live Truman." Others read "We do not want Communism." The crowd lacked the terrifying, monotonous order of a Communist demonstration, and small groups were singing "God Bless America" and waving to the employees peering from Consulate windows.

It was ironic that within a year and a few months crowds were again marching past the American Consulate in Budapest—only this time they carried red flags and banners reading "Down with America," "Down with Truman" and "Long Live Stalin." It was small consolation to think that some of these dejected Red marchers had several months before sung "God Bless America" under our windows.

Sometime later, crowds of Communist marchers could be seen marching through Budapest carrying placards reading "Death to Bela Kovacs" (a leader of the Smallholders Party) and other persons who were in disfavor with the Communist Party. When I first saw these death placards, I didn't attach great significance to them. It was only when Bela Kovacs was actually taken by the political police and summarily executed that I began to notice that the placards foretold with terrible accuracy the fate of those Hungarians who dared to openly oppose the Communists.

I saw conditions in Hungary grow progressively worse from 1945 to 1950. It seemed that each year the Communists grew bolder in their campaign of terror to isolate the country from the West and stamp out every spark of potential resistance.

American and other foreign citizens were arrested on charges which were not only false but actually ludicrous.

Consular officers were not permitted to see or communi-
cate with their imprisoned citizens. Finally, realizing that it
was not in a position to protect its citizens, the United
States Government prohibited their travel in Hungary. The
atrocities of the Red Army had been replaced by the brutal
terror of the Hungarian Communist Security Police.

One day a young Hungarian messenger at the Consulate
was inducted into the army. We learned a few weeks later
that he had been executed because he had tried to teach
English to some of his friends in the barracks. He was
charged with being a "spy" for the Americans.

The huge concentration camps, of which there are many
in Hungary, were already filled with "enemies of the People's Democracy" in 1948. By the following year it was
necessary to put the camp inmates to work enlarging their
prisons.

Many of my friends were in these prisons at Kistarcsa,
South-Buda and Vac—placed there without any trials or
hearings whatsoever. One of my acquaintances was taken
from his home in Budapest one evening in 1948. The two
plainclothesmen who called for him told his wife and little
daughter that he was needed to sign some real estate
documents and would be back within the hour. He has
never been seen nor heard from since.

Communism made no distinction as to the racial and
religious background of its enemies. Jews, Catholics and
Protestants alike made up the population of the Communist concentration camps in Hungary. Several of my Jewish
acquaintances returned to Budapest from Nazi concentration camps in Germany and were imprisoned by the Communists at Kistarcsa.

My last two years in Hungary were, to say the least, not
pleasant. The personnel of the "Western" legations and

consulates in Budapest found themselves ostracised by the majority of the local population. This was understandable because those Hungarians who were known to be on friendly terms with the Americans and British soon found themselves in the hands of the Communist Security Police.

Old Hungarian friends whom I had known for years could not risk being seen with me in public. Many times when I met them strolling down crowded Vaci street, they would turn and look into a shop window. I understood.

During my last year in Hungary I rented a house in Buda. The house was almost constantly under surveillance by plainclothesmen of the security police. I returned home many nights at 12:00 or 1:00 o'clock and found a man standing under a street lamp near by the house pretending to read a newspaper. The police were extremely interested in knowing which Hungarians visited me or spoke with me.

I do not wish to give the impression that I was the only "Westerner" under the prying eyes of the Communist police. The foreign personnel of all of the Western legations and consulates were continually shadowed—even when going out for an evening at a night club or theater.

Watching for and guarding against Communist traps eventually becomes second nature to our Legation and Consular personnel in the Iron Curtain countries. During recent years the Communist governments have been looking for every possible opportunity to brand a "Westerner" as an Imperialist Spy or Saboteur. It was common practice for them to "plant" incriminating documents or other phony evidence so that it could be "discovered" by their Security Police in possession of a western diplomat or consular employee—who, if he was a foreigner, was expelled from the country amid the loud rejoicing of the local press and the Moscow propaganda machine. I never entered my automobile to drive downtown before having carefully inspected every possible place where such "documents" could have been hidden.

These attempted Communist traps reached such fantastic proportions in 1950 that one of them attempted to involve me in the tragic Mindszenty affair. One afternoon a shabbily dressed individual called at my office at the Consulate and requested to speak with me urgently and privately. He sat down in my office and showed me a small card identifying him as the driver of the police truck used in the transport of prisoners from the infamous Andrassy ut 60 Communist prison in Budapest to a concentration camp in the country. When I expressed surprise that he should come to see me, he whispered:

Yes, I have risked my life coming here. But I was sent by Mrs. _____, who is a close friend of yours, and who is now a Communist prisoner at Andrassy 60. I am actually a devout Catholic. Mrs. _____ entrusted me with your plans to liberate Cardinal Mindszenty from prison and told me to see you, and that you would let me know how I could be of assistance."

I ushered him out of my office.

The Communists in Hungary made life miserable for Americans there in many other small ways. It soon became impossible to spend a weekend at Lake Lillafured, one of the most beautiful spots in Hungary, because the local hotel was invariably taken over by Communist groups. In previous years it had been customary for villagers in Lillafured to rent rooms to tourists when the hotel was filled. However, when I applied for rooms at several houses in the village, I was told that none was available. One villager told me quite frankly that he wouldn't dare risk renting a room to an American.

Austro-Hungarian Border

In order that this record may be reasonably complete, I must also jot down some notes about the Austro-Hungarian border and the Hungarian Communist police who guarded it. The Hungarians, of course, did not guard it against a potential Austrian invasion, since the Austrian territory along the Hungarian border was in the Russian zone of occupation. It was guarded against escaping Hungarians fleeing to the western zones of Austria and Germany.

As early as 1947, the Hungarians began to strengthen this border guard. A person viewing for the first time the border area at any of the principal roadways got the immediate impression that he was entering or leaving a huge state prison—depending upon which way he was travelling.

I drove to Vienna from Budapest several times each month, usually crossing the border at Hegyeshalom. I was always stopped at least three or four times by policemen on the highway even before I neared the border. These policemen, who were changed frequently, usually wore the uniform of the Security Police, which was brown khaki, very similar to a Russian officer's uniform. They always demanded to see my documents and looked into the car to see if there was anyone hiding there. They patrolled the highway in pairs, and while one examined the car and the documents, the other stood in front of the car with his rifle or tommy-gun at the ready.

Upon arriving at the customs house at the border, one was usually greeted by several security policemen, some of whom were deployed on both sides of the highway with their tommy-guns trained on the automobile. Under this

guard, the car's occupants were shown into the new concrete building housing the passport and customs
inspectors.

After the passport was stamped, the customs man usually asked to see the spare tire, using this as a pretext to see
if anyone was hiding in the trunk of the car.

Near the customs house was a tower, resembling an oil
well derrick, with a huge searchlight on top. There was also
a man on top of the tower scanning the area with field
glasses. Similar towers were set up at regular intervals all
along the Austro-Hungarian border, and all trees and
underbrush were cleared for a width of a quarter of a mile
on the Hungarian side of the border. In addition, two rows
of barbed wire were stretched along the Hungarian side,
and land mines were planted between these rows of wire
entanglements. As if this were not enough to discourage
those fleeing from Communism, the entire border was
patrolled by Hungarian border policemen accompanied by
trained dogs which looked like bloodhounds.

Even with all of these barriers, many Hungarians still
managed to slip across to the western zones of Austria.
Many more failed to get across and were either killed or
sent to prison.

Near the end of my sojourn in Hungary, I was the acci-
dental witness to a silent drama near Hegyeshalom which I
shall note here. One morning in early 1950, I had just had
my passport stamped and driven past the Hungarian customs building toward Vienna, when I noticed a strange
procession coming across a field from the direction of the
Austrian custom house. I drove as slowly as possible, without stopping, in order to see what was happening.

An old man, an old woman, a youth of about 20 and a
young girl not more than 12 years old, with knapsacks

strapped to their backs were being marched toward the highway by four husky Hungarian Security Policemen and a Russian soldier, all armed with tommy-guns. When the old man's steps faltered, he was jabbed in the back with the muzzle of the gun in the policeman's hands. The old woman and the young girl were crying. Then, as they neared the highway, a thrilling and amazing thing happened. Whether the old man recognized my car as an American car or whether he saw the small American flag on the windshield, I will never know. But he stopped—looked directly at the car and raised his right hand with his first two fingers extended in the V-sign. V for Victory.

Special thanks for the "Preface" to
   Stephen R. Dujack
   Worldwatch Institute
      former Editor of the *Foreign Service Journal*

Short lyrical excerpts are from:
   "Shall We Gather at the River"
      Robert Lowry, 1864
   "Kiss Me Again"
      Henry Blossom, 1905, music by Victor Herbert
      Copyright 1915, Warner Bros. Inc. (Renewed)
      All rights reserved, used by permission

- design and graphic production by John R. Kirschner
- typeset in Souvenir by Comp-Type, Inc.,
      Fort Bragg, California
- printed on Howard Permalife, a non-acid paper by
      The Robots, Inc., Palo Alto, California
- binding by Special Editions, Stockton, California